Conversations with Cosmo

To Katie

With affection

from Betty Jean & Cosmo

AT HOME WITH AN
AFRICAN GREY PARROT

By Betty Jean Craige

Preface by Irene Pepperberg

SHERMAN ASHER PUBLISHING   ·   Santa Fe

ISBN 13: 978-1890932-374-1
Library of Congress Control Number: 2009943897

Cover design by Maureen Burdock
Edited by Cinny Green
Text design by Jim Mafchir
Photo Credits: John Ahee and Robert Newcomb

Sherman Asher Publishing
P.O. Box 31752
Santa Fe, NM 87594-1725

www.shermanasher.com   westernedge@santa-fe.net

*I dedicate this book
to Margaret and Wyatt Anderson,
Cosmo's extended human family.*

Acknowledgments

I thank Judith Ortiz Cofer, brilliant writer and good friend, for inspiring me to write this book and providing helpful criticism of it. Judy's students love her as a teacher, and now I know why.

I thank Julie Dingus, with whom I've worked at the Willson Center for Humanities and Arts at the University of Georgia for some ten years, for reading the manuscript carefully and thoughtfully. Julie shares my sense of humor, and she let me know what she thought was funny, to my great gratification.

I thank my brother Branch Craige and my colleagues Hugh Ruppersburg and Nicole Mitchell for reading critically the whole manuscript and responding to it with good suggestions.

I thank my many other wonderful friends not only for reading parts or all of the chapters but also for listening patiently to my Cosmo stories over the years and receiving with apparent enthusiasm the numerous email "Cosmo updates" I sent them regularly to brag about my parrot's latest achievements.

I thank Lloyd Winstead, my other companion at the Willson Center, for welcoming Cosmo on her many visits to my office. I thank Margaret and Wyatt Anderson,

Richard Neupert, Cathy Jones, Sophie Neupert, Doris Kadish, and Raymond Woller for entertaining Cosmo frequently in their homes. And I thank all my colleagues who have given Cosmo work experience by inviting her to their classes and book clubs.

I thank John Ahee and Robert Newcomb for taking good pictures of Cosmo and me. John Ahee's picture of Cosmo giving me an affectionate peck on the nose is on the book's cover.

I thank John Avise, geneticist, ornithologist, bird photographer, and parakeet lover, for taking me to the pet store in May of 2002 to show me baby Cosmo.

I thank Jim Mafchir of Sherman Asher Publishing for his interest in Cosmo and for his confidence in this book about her. And I thank Cynthia Green for being a superb editor, and Maureen Burdock for designing the striking cover.

I thank Cosmo for being a good bird and my dogs Mary and Kaylee for not eating her.

Contents

Preface

*H*aving anything to do with parrots evokes many conflicting emotions. As someone who has studied them for over thirty years and who has interacted with them in some manner for almost my entire life, I am well aware of their engaging personalities and the considerable joy that they can bring to their human companions. I am, of course, also aware of the noise, the mess, and the responsibilities that accepting these birds into one's life engenders. And, although I fortunately have had little firsthand experience with the negative side of the parrot trade, I am also aware of the sad plight of large numbers of parrots whose owners abuse them, whether through neglect or more active forms of negative behavior, of the equally large numbers of parrots that end up at shelters and sanctuaries as a consequence, and of some of the less-than-sterling breeders who have little care for the birds themselves other than as money-making stock. That is why I am so glad that Betty Jean Craige has written this book.

Professor Craige describes in great detail the intelligence and the striking personality of her Grey parrot, Cosmo. Craige entertains us with many anecdotes that provide insights into a brain that, although organized somewhat differently from those of mammals, functions

11

in ways reminiscent of a young child. Cosmo clearly analyzes situations, uses her relatively limited vocal vocabulary, and devises appropriate communicative strategies to get what she wants in many varied situations, be it a special treat or just some additional attention. But Craige also explains to us just how Cosmo has developed into such a wonderful being: it is Craige's constant interactions with Cosmo, their immersion in one another's lives, and the fact that Craige treats Cosmo as one would treat an inquisitive toddler.

Thus Professor Craige does not make light of the responsibility she has undertaken in bringing Cosmo into her life. We learn about their daily routines, of Cosmo's endless craving for close, personal attention, and even of Craige's awareness of the need to figure out how to provide for Cosmo when she is no longer capable of so doing. Craige doesn't spare us the descriptions of the bird-food littered floor, of the feathers that get into all possible nooks and crannies, the occasional painful bites, the destruction of anything that Cosmo might consider beak-worthy (whether it be a designated parrot toy or a valuable antique), the expense and work needed to provide a diet that is more varied and probably better than that of the average American human, and the times when maybe a bit more peace and quiet would be appreciated. Craige, albeit with a light touch, makes it clear that parrots are not creatures that provide unconditional love and that they are clearly not good companions for folks who are unwilling to make the same kind of effort and sacrifices that she does.

So enjoy the truly wonderful stories about Cosmo— of her interacting with Professor Craige, with the dogs with whom she shares a house, with Craige's dinner guests and family, of the tricks Cosmo plays on her companions (human and canine)—but remember that such an exceptional bird requires an equally exceptional owner.

—Irene M. Pepperberg, author of
The Alex Studies and *Alex and Me.*

1. Where Wanna Gonna Go?

COSMO: *"Where wanna gonna go?"*
BJC: *"Betty Jean wanna go to work."*
COSMO: *"Cosmo wanna go to work, okay?"*
BJC: *"No. Cosmo stay home. Cosmo stay home with doggies."*
COSMO: *"Okay. Doggies! Come here!" [Cosmo whistles.]*
BJC: *"Good-bye. I love you."*
COSMO: *"Good-bye. I love you. Betty Jean be back soon, okay?"*

*S*o goes a typical morning conversation with Cosmo, my eight-year-old female African Grey Parrot. Cosmo, who initiated this particular exchange one day in the fall of 2008, was watching me prepare to leave the house for the University of Georgia. Having been to my office and having accompanied me to classes—my own class in ecocriticism and other classes in psychology, anthropology, speech communication, philosophy, and ornithology—Cosmo knew what work was. Work entailed going "in a car" and meeting "company," who would talk about her and to her, whistle with her, and laugh at her jokes. For her, work was fun. She would be happy to go to work every day.

Cosmo had long before invented the phrase "Where wanna gonna go?" She had uttered some one hundred words and two hundred phrases by the age of six, when I stopped keeping track. I stopped keeping track because her ability to make her own sentences, all meaningful though not all syntactically correct, had turned her in my mind into a feathery little person. I converse with her naturally and affectionately, almost unthinkingly, albeit in simplified speech patterns and with limited vocabulary.

Only occasionally now do I feel the amazement I first felt when I witnessed a one-year-old Cosmo trying to communicate with me in my language. But when I have company in the living room and see the efforts Cosmo makes to contribute to the merriment, from a cage around the corner in the dining room, I realize that Cosmo is an extraordinary animal. She competes with the laughing and talking guests to bring attention to herself, and she does so effectively, very effectively, by whistling, speaking, and laughing uproariously at her own humor. That is how she makes friends. That is how she gets us to love her.

Cosmo likes attention. And she deserves attention, for she enables all of us who know her—and she has many friends indeed in Athens, Georgia, where we live— to reconsider our understanding of the intelligence of non-human species. I have written this book, *Conversations with Cosmo: At Home with an African Grey Parrot*, to share with readers everywhere the story of Cosmo's development as a talking bird. To bring you into her life, I have recreated many of the conversations Cosmo and I have had, conversations I would describe as usual and normal. Of course, as in human discourse, no conversation replicates a previous conversation exactly, but every one of these conversations has taken place at one time or another, and most of them have taken place with slight variations numerous times.

Cosmo is now quite a conversationalist—for a bird—as you will see. Most African Greys, males and females alike, have the ability to talk intelligibly. But, contrary to common opinion, so do a number of other parrots. Greg, my handyman and friend, had entertained me for years with stories about his Blue and Gold

Macaw, Boo Boo, whom he and his wife Jacqueline had adopted when the bird's owners divorced. Boo Boo, said Greg, came to his new home with three voices: a man's voice, a woman's voice, and a whisper—presumably the voice of one of them speaking quietly on the phone, maybe to a lover. When Boo Boo got in trouble, he would screech "Help!" or "Mama!" or, if Jacqueline failed to come right away, "Mother!" Greg's stories inspired me to get Cosmo.

I chose the name "Cosmo" for my baby African Grey because nobody I knew had that name. Although I had read that male and female Greys were indistinguishable from each other, I somehow thought that I had a male. Not until two years later did I learn from her veterinarian, who ran a DNA test on her, that Cosmo was a female. By then she was referring to herself as Cosmo—or Cos—and I didn't want to give her a new name.

When I brought Cosmo home from a local pet store, on May 31, 2002, I knew that I would learn from her. I had always been fascinated by language acquisition in non-human animals, having read stories about Koko the gorilla, Lana the chimpanzee, and Akeakamai the bottlenose dolphin, whom I introduced to my students in discussions of the influence of language on intellectual capacity. Some thirty-five years ago I read *Language, Thought, and Reality*, in which Benjamin Lee Whorf argued that an individual's—or a society's—understanding of the world, including time and space, was conditioned by language. Since then I had wondered whether the acquisition of a human language by a non-human animal would give the animal a conceptual framework the animal would not have had otherwise. The work in the 1970s at the Yerkes National Primate

Research Centre at Emory University by my friend Ernst von Glasersfeld and his colleague Duane Rumbaugh with the chimp Lana seemed to support this theory. Using a computer, Lana learned to make novel utterances with lexigrams. At Stanford University, Koko, who communicated with humans using more than 1,000 signs in American Sign Language and comprehended 2,000 spoken words in English, used language to lie to humans and to joke.

I figured that an African Grey Parrot (*Psittacus erithacus*), known for high intelligence and the ability to mimic human speech, would teach me about language acquisition up close and personal. Perhaps human language would enable Cosmo to communicate her thoughts to me. So in response to questions about why I had gotten a parrot, I said that it seemed easier than getting a gorilla, a chimp, or a dolphin. I also said that if I, at the age of fifty-six, was ever to have a zoo I'd better get started.

Cosmo is a Congo African Grey, with the typical crimson tail feathers and all black beak. She weighs about a pound. There are two subspecies of African Grey Parrots: the Congo African Grey, from the lowland tropical forests and mangroves of Central Africa, and the smaller Timneh African Grey, from West Africa, which has a darker gray body, maroon tail feathers, and paler beak. Reportedly, they exhibit similar intelligence and similar speaking ability, and they are equally sociable. Cosmo is not a wild-caught parrot, I hasten to say, for wild-caught parrots are unhappy in captivity. Cosmo was hatched in Florida, from several generations of Floridians, and she has lived with humans and other animals her entire life.

When I bought Cosmo I didn't know how much I would come to love her. In May of 2002 my household included four American Eskimo Dogs I loved, Holly, Blanche, Daisy, and Kaylee, renowned locally for their images on my annual Christmas cards. I had already raised the dogs' curiosity when I outfitted my house— their house—with three large bird cages (22" x 24" x 53," playscape on top), which I'd ordered the day I chose Cosmo, three weeks before she could eat on her own and depart her pet store caregivers. Thus when I extracted Cosmo from the dog crate I'd used to bring her home that summer afternoon, Holly, Blanche, Daisy, and Kaylee were exceedingly curious. They sniffed her respectfully as she perched self-confidently on my left hand under protection by my right, and made her acquaintance. Cosmo showed little fear of them, for she had met many dogs, cats, ferrets, rabbits, hamsters, and birds, as well as people, during her stay at the pet store. I took Cosmo into the sunroom, where she would have her roost cage. There, in a room of her own, she would be able to watch the squirrels, chipmunks, and birds feeding on the deck outside her window.

I had only one frightening moment on the first evening. While I was teaching her to "step up," Cosmo stepped down, off my hand, and flew—sort of—under the bed, where Kaylee was hiding in her lair. I'll never forget lying on the floor, squeezing under the bed to reach Cosmo, and staring into the eyes of what looked then like a hungry little white fox two feet away from my precious baby parrot. Meanwhile Holly, Blanche, and Daisy all poked their noses under the bed to find out what was happening. Cosmo returned to me, quickly.

Actually, I need not have worried about the dogs eating Cosmo, because the dogs became wary of her beak immediately, or almost immediately. Perhaps there was a beak-bite or two on a furry paw or two before everybody settled down. Within a month or so of her arrival, the dogs and Cosmo were comfortable enough with each other that Cosmo could be out of her cage whenever I was home to supervise. Supervision meant protecting the house from Cosmo, rather than protecting Cosmo from the dogs. Obviously, from the look of my baseboards and wood trim around the doors and windows, I haven't been a very good supervisor. But no matter: I've been a fine companion animal.

Like all African Greys, Cosmo did not talk until she was a year old, in December of 2002. But throughout that summer and fall, we whistled to each other. She would wolf-whistle *whee whew*, and I would repeat it, to let her know that we were communicating. She would whistle whee whee whew, and I would copy that. Then she would whistle *whee whee whee whew*, and I would whistle whee whee whee whee whew, and she would whistle *whee whee whee whee whee whew,* and we would go on like this until she tired of the game and whistled *whee whee whee whee whee whee whee whee whew whew*! Once she got up to thirteen *whees* before the *whew*. Now when I say *whee whew* to her she says, "Thank you." I taught her that.

Later we played the same game with words:

COSMO: "Cosmo is a good bird!"
BJC: "Cosmo is a good good bird."
COSMO: "Cosmo is a good good good good good bird!"

With another whistle I customarily used for calling the dogs, Cosmo would call me, and the dogs, to her cage. The dogs obeyed her twice before they realized they owed no obeisance to a bird. I obeyed her a lot more often than that. Cosmo experimented with a variety of fancy whistles, and still does, and I copied them faithfully. At one point an observant friend asked which one of us was the parrot.

Cosmo also mimicked just about every sound the house made. From her cage in the dining room, at the entrance to the kitchen, Cosmo would watch my dinner preparations with great interest. She had lived with me no more than two months before she could imitate the beeps from the microwave and the oven and the squeaks from the cabinet doors. A split second before I opened a cabinet door, she would make the appropriate squeak. And if I approached the door to my garage, which has a very loud, very distinctive, very prolonged *squeeeeeeak,* she would announce my departure a full two seconds before my hand touched the doorknob.

Having grown up in El Paso, Texas, I get a hankering for Mexican food every so often, so I bring home fresh serrano chili peppers and put them under the broiler to burn the skins off. The scent of the roasting peppers is heavenly, as anybody who lives on the border knows, but the blare of the smoke alarm is not. It's more like hellish. One August afternoon, when the peppers started burning, the alarm went on—and I ran around opening windows and doors to let the smoke escape. Cosmo must have delighted in all the excitement, for she would remember the effect of the sound on my actions.

In October, when I repeated the exercise with a new set of chili peppers, as soon as the scent of the burning peppers started wafting through the kitchen, I heard the smoke alarm. Again I ran around opening windows and doors to let the smoke escape—but there was no smoke. The ear-splitting signal continued, so I wondered if it was coming from Cosmo. I looked at her. Silence. I looked away and heard the signal again. I looked at her; she looked at me, very still, perching innocently on top of her cage, which was right by the smoke alarm. So I removed the alarm from the wall, took it to the other side of the kitchen, and waited. Sure enough: When I turned my back to her, Cosmo mimicked the signal perfectly at the appropriate decibel level. She had associated the scent of the roasting peppers with the shrill sound of the alarm. When I whirled around to confront her, she shut up. Nowadays, she'd give herself away by laughing and saying, "That's Cosmo!" Then, at the age of ten months, she neither talked nor laughed. She just imitated sounds.

Cosmo learned to mimic the tiny *peep* of dying smoke alarm batteries. You can imagine my frustration over trying to determine whether the peep sounding at the aggravating five-minute intervals was emitted by one of the smoke alarms—and by which one?—or by Cosmo.

Cosmo learned to mimic the ring of the telephone so accurately that she could pull me out of the shower or in from outside to race to the phone. I could not tell the difference between Cosmo's *rrrring* and the phone's *rrrring* unless I was in another room with another phone that was not ringing. To this day she continues to *rrrring* the phone whenever she wants me to drop what I'm doing and come to her. But now she confesses: "That's Cosmo! *Hahahaha*."

One Saturday, she would not stop making a per-plexing and highly annoying *bleep* at one-second inter-vals. My naturalist neighbors Jim and Nelle, who watch over our woods and know where every woodpecker, hawk, fox, deer, squirrel, and raccoon lives, figured it out. Cosmo was mimicking the sound of a truck backing up during the construction of a sewer easement behind my house, construction that did not go on during the weekend. Cosmo mimics every sound she finds interesting.

Later, while cooking dinner, I deleted forty caller IDs from my kitchen phone. *Bip bip* times forty. When I finished the task, Cosmo continued the bips for another four long minutes: "*Bip bip, bip bip, bip bip, bip bip, bip bip . . . .*"

Of course Cosmo learned to mimic the dogs' bark: "*Woo woo woo!*" And the different chirps of the many species of birds in the woods behind the house: Carolina wrens, finches, sparrows, chickadees, blue jays, cardinals, crows, doves, hawks, and woodpeckers.

Does Cosmo mimic these environmental noises for amusement's sake? Is the mimicry a form of play for her? I wonder.

In January of 2003, at about thirteen months, Cosmo started repeating the phrases I had been saying to her since I got her: "Hello!" "Hi!" "Wanna peanut?" which she intones as a request. For a while we would get stuck in the cycle of my asking, "Hello. How are you?" Cosmo responded, "Fine, thank you, how are you?" and I responded, "Fine, thank you, how are you?" She then responded, "Fine, thank you, how are you?" and on and on.

Soon she was uttering her name in front of "wanna," as in "Cosmo wanna peanut," "Cosmo wanna water," "Cosmo wanna be a good bird." And she began saying, at the right moments and sometimes out of the blue, "I love you."

My 2003 holiday card was accompanied by a letter in which I listed Cosmo's utterances of the previous twelve months. They were:

Hello Hi How are you? Fine Here are you? Here I am! I am here! What are you doing? What doing? Up Wanna go up Go up here Wanna go up here

Come here! Ow! There you are! I love you Wanna kiss Thank you No! No, No, bad! ball Play ball *Woo woo* Cosmo What's that? Goodbye Bye Bye, Cosmo Wanna cuddle? Wanna peanut Peanut Bird Cosmo is a bird Cosmo is a good bird Good bird! Wanna peanut Wow! Come here Come up here Step up What do you want? Wanna peanut No, no more No more peanut I love you

That Christmas Eve, I brought to our traditional dinner party at Jan's an audio tape I had recorded of Cosmo talking to herself early in the morning. It was forty-five minutes of words, whistles, squeaks, environmental noises, and silences that went something like this:

Hello *Chirp* Hi *Woo woo woo* How are you? Fine *Whee whew* Here are you? Here I am! I am here! Squeeeeeeak What are you doing? *Beep . . . beep* What doing? *Chee chee* Up Wanna go up *Hooo hooo* [Silence...] Go up here Wanna go up here Click Come here! Ow! There you are! I love you Wanna kiss Thank you *Bip bip* No! No, no, bad! Caw caw Ball Play ball *Woo woo* Cosmo What's that? Goodbye Bye Bye, Cosmo [Silence...] Wanna cuddle? *Tweet tweet* Wanna peanut Peanut *Squeeeeeeeak* Bird Cosmo is a bird *Chirrup chirrup* Cosmo is a good bird Good bird! *Whee whee whee whew* Wanna peanut Wow! *Caw caw* Come here Come up here Step up [Long silence...] *Whee whee whew* What do you want? Wanna peanut *Woo woo woo woo* No, no more No more peanut *Rrrring* I love you

I loved the whole forty-five minutes of that tape, so I put it on the tape player I'd brought for the other guests to hear. Everybody seemed to be listening attentively, but when I left the room briefly, something must have happened to the tape because when I got back it had disappeared and Arlo Guthrie's "Alice's Restaurant" had replaced it.

> You can get anything you want at Alice's Restau-
> rant
> You can get anything you want at Alice's Restau-
> rant
> Walk right in it's around the back . . .

For the life of me, I can't see why my friends found those lyrics more appealing than Cosmo's adorable utterances.

About this time my nephew Branch and his soon-to-be wife Siobhan, who were in graduate school at Emory University and who—I'm happy to say—showed interest in every single one of Cosmo's adorable utterances, alerted me to Irene Pepperberg's groundbreaking book *The Alex Studies*, which Branch had read in a psychology course. Irene Pepperberg, who had earned a PhD in Chemical Physics from Harvard University in 1979, had shifted her scholarly interests while writing her dissertation from chemistry to animal behavior and had subsequently done remarkable research on an African Grey she had named Alex (acronym for "Avian Learning Experiment"). *The Alex Studies*, published in 1999, changed the scientific community's assessment of "the cognitive and communicative abilities of grey parrots," just as the 1995 video *Alex the Grey in Training Sessions with Professor Irene Pepperberg*, seen by millions of television viewers, had previously changed the public's view of bird brains. When he died unexpectedly in 2007, Alex received obituaries in *The New York Times*, *The Economist*, and major newspapers and magazines around the world. The news release issued by Brandeis University, where Alex had lived in Irene's laboratory, told the story of Irene's and Alex's accomplishment.

> WALTHAM, MA (SEPTEMBER 10, 2007)—Alex, the world renowned African Grey parrot made famous by the ground-breaking cognition and communication research conducted by Irene Pepperberg, Ph.D., died at the age of 31 on September 6, 2007. Dr. Pepperberg's pioneering research resulted in Alex learning elements of English speech to identify 50 different objects, 7 colors, 5 shapes, quantities up to and including 6 and a zero-like concept. He used phrases such as "I want X" and "Wanna go Y", where X and Y were appropriate object and location labels. He acquired concepts of categories, bigger and smaller, same-different, and absence. Alex combined his labels to identify, request, refuse, and categorize more than 100 different items demonstrating a level and scope of cognitive abilities never expected in an avian species. Pepperberg says that Alex showed the emotional equivalent of a 2 year-old child and intellectual equivalent of a 5 year-old. Her research with Alex shattered the generally held notion that parrots are only capable of mindless vocal mimicry.

Parrot lovers owe Irene Pepperberg, who is now a friend of mine, a huge debt of gratitude for her work, and so do parrots, for they may get better treatment from us humans now that we understand their capacity for thought and feeling.

Nine years before Alex's death, Irene said to David Chandler of the Boston Globe on May 18, 1998, that she would not claim that Alex had language. She said, "You could never have the kind of conversation with him that you would have with another person—a two-way conversation. But he can tell us what he wants, and answer questions posed to him." Irene expresses the caution of

Irene Pepperberg and Cosmo, in Betty Jean's home.

a scientist in her reluctance to claim that Alex had acquired language. I am less reluctant. From my perspective, Alex and Cosmo both acquired language—English— and that language enabled them to have two-way conversations with their human companions. Irene's marvelous memoir *Alex and Me* displays Alex's astonishing ability to comprehend verbal interactions, to manipulate his people using English, and to have fun using the conceptual skills that Irene had taught him.

Cosmo is not unlike Alex in her language capacity. When Cosmo asks me, "Where wanna gonna go?" she knows that I am getting ready to leave the house. She never asks that question when I'm taking a Sunday afternoon nap on the sofa in her room, or cooking up a Saturday night feast in the kitchen, or cuddling with her in front of the television, or taking a shower at bedtime. And when she asks a question, any question, she wants an answer. When I answer we have a two-way conversation, an exchange of information.

And when Cosmo answers a question I have asked her, we have a two-way conversation as well. On a Sunday morning when a woodpecker was hacking away at my house, I asked her, "What's that?" Cosmo listened and replied, "That's a birdy!"

I have not given Cosmo the academic education Irene gave Alex, nor have I studied Cosmo scientifically. I am leaving that scientific project to Erin Colbert-White, a graduate student in psychology at the University of Georgia who has written her Master's thesis on Cosmo's language use. However, I have given Cosmo a busy social life, and as a result, in my view, she has developed social skills: an ability to ask for things, such as peanuts, in my language; an ability to use my language to acquire information; a sensitivity to the moods of people around her; a recognition of appropriate means of interaction with others, human and canine; and a sense of humor.

I often wonder whether Greys in the wild have a sense of humor. I do know that they live in large flocks of hundreds, sometimes thousands, of birds—all Greys—and that they are extremely sensitive to each other's actions. In other words, they exhibit flock behavior, whereby the whole flock seems to think as one. Greys are prey, and by flying together and feeding together they can depend on their flock-mates to sound the alert when a predator approaches. Because they feed on the ground, as well as in the canopy, they must have quick reflexes. I found out from my trusty handbook, *African Grey Parrots* by Maggie Wright, that African Grey chicks are fairly slow maturing and that they stay in their

A flock of wild African Grey Parrots (Photo courtesy AfriPics)

small family units of five or six birds until they are a year or so, during which time they learn from their parents and other older birds how to survive. I suspect that their extended period of immaturity enables Greys, when bred as pets, to adapt easily to their human, wordy, environment. They learn from us humans, who serve as their parents when they are chicks and as their family unit later on, how to navigate a social situation successfully, how to talk, and when to laugh. They learn from us humans what is funny—at least, what is funny to us.

· · ·

For Borders Books and Music Educators Weekend on October 4, 2008, a former student of mine who is now a manager at the Athens store, invited me to speak there about language acquisition in African Grey Parrots and to bring Cosmo with me. I felt honored to receive the in-

31

vitation, and I accepted it, for I never turn down an opportunity to show people how intelligent Cosmo is. On that Saturday afternoon while driving with her across town, I told Cosmo, "We're gonna talk with company!" When we arrived, a store employee and I placed her travel cage on a bench in a spacious area towards the back. About twenty-five children and twenty-five adults showed up to hear Cosmo say, well, almost nothing. Maybe "Cosmo wanna peanut" every so often, and "Cosmo wanna go up," but not much more. I was frustrated, but I chatted about Cosmo's language ability and answered questions while the children crowded about Cosmo's cage. That was the problem, in fact. Cosmo was surrounded by inquisitive children who loomed large above her. Since she prefers being high up where she's safe, she did not demonstrate her verbal abilities.

Meanwhile, a photographer from the *Athens Banner Herald* was taking lots of pictures with a fancy camera, and a reporter was taking notes. A week later the Sunday morning paper carried a lovely story with glorious photos that made Cosmo famous in Athens for forty-eight hours or so. But the next day the paper carried a not-so-lovely letter to the editor criticizing the paper for encouraging "the capture, sale and captivity of these once-wild birds" and accusing parrot-owners like me of selfishly displaying these animals for our own pleasure. I didn't answer that letter, but I thought about it.

I agree that we should desist in the capturing of wild birds—everywhere. But keeping domestically bred pet birds is not, in my opinion, a sin. I have come to believe that the responsible ownership of parrots can serve well both parrots and humans. Our civilization has misunderstood and underestimated the African Grey Parrots' ability to talk, think, feel, tell jokes, and amuse themselves. Over the centuries, many humans have kept these remarkable animals for personal pleasure, and many have displayed them without regard to the parrots' sensitivities, certainly. But many other humans have given their pet parrots pleasure in return, as we are ethically obliged to do to compensate them for the absence of the excitement they would have had in the jungle.

I hope that our discovery of their intelligence, which we are gaining through relationships with individual parrots, will reinforce our respect for our non-human fellow residents of the earth and will make us better citizens of the global biotic community. I hope that it will also make us more ethical farmers and fishermen and more responsible keepers of the wild.

The day after she did not speak at Borders Books and Music, Cosmo spoke at Oconee County Elementary School, a public school in the Athens area, to a class of third-graders. Perched safely atop her travel cage, which we had placed on a table, Cosmo looked down at forty admiring eight-year-old humans sitting on the floor and said, "Cosmo wanna go to work," and the children laughed. Then she laughed, and crowed, "Cosmo is a bird!" They laughed again. Then she told them her jokes: "Telephone for bird!" and "You have reached Cosmo!" The children whistled to her, and Cosmo whistled back. "*Whee whew!*" Cosmo thoroughly enjoyed being with the children, and the children thoroughly enjoyed being with her. That day, the third-graders all learned a lesson for life: that animals, like them, are smart.

2. Cosmo Wanna Kiss

COSMO: "*Hi How are you? Here are you? Fine Here I am!
I am here! Yoohoo What are you doing? What doing? Up
Wanna go up Go up here Wanna go up here Come here! Ow!
That hurt! Bad bird! There you are! I love you Wanna kiss
Kiss for B'Jean? Thank you No! No, no, Bad! Ball Play ball
Woo woo! That's bark That's barking Barkybark Cosmo
Cosmo is a good bird What's that? Goodbye Bye Wanna
cuddle Wanna peanut Peanut Bird Cosmo is a bird Cosmo
is a good bird Good bird! Wow! Cosmo is a good good good
bird! Come here Come up here Step up What do you want?
What's that? No, no more No more peanut Wanna kiss No,
no more kiss Whaaaaay–That's water Wanna water How are
you? Fine, thank you Wanna shower I wanna kiss What?
Wanna shower Cosmo is a good good bird Cosmo wanna good
kiss Come Come on What? Yes Okay Wanna cuddle
Cosmo wanna peanut Cosmo wanna be a good bird Wanna
poop Oh good bird! Good morning Wanna apple Bad bird–
back in cage Wanna be a good bird Wanna dance? Wanna go
back in cage No, no, no! Where are you? Good bye–Hafta
leave? Stay here! Birdy Cosmo is a birdy Cosmo is a good
birdy Feathers Cosmo has feathers Birdy has feathers
What's Cosmo? Cosmo is a birdy What's Cosmo? Cosmo is a
bird Wanna go to kitchen? Shower for B'Jean? Shower for
bird Feathers for Cosmo Clothes Clothes for B'Jean B'Jean
has clothes Yes Yeeas! Company! We're gonna have company? Wanna company Wanna company for Cosmo Move!
OK, move Where wanna wanna go? Water for B' Jean Clothes
for B'Jean That's Cosmo Bird Telephone for Cosmo! Telephone for Bird!-- Hehehehehehe Telephone for B'Jean! We're
gonna have company! Wanna dance? Wanna dance Hafta
wanna go to work? B'Jean wanna work? Cosmo wanna
work!–Hehehehehe Hehehehehe–That's funny! You've reached
706935----Telephone! B'Jean wanna dance? B'Jean hafta go*

35

to work? Where wanna go? Wanna go to bed! Cosmo wanna go to bed Time to go to bed Good night B'Jean wanna come here? Wanna orange Wanna go up Cosmo is a fine bird Cosmo is a good good good good bird! Cosmo is a good good fine bird! Fur Ow!–That hurt Come here! Where we're gonna go? That's whistle Hello how are you–That's talk Woo woo woo–That's bark That's barky bark Doggies! Doggy bark Wanna walk? Cosmo wanna walk!–Hehehehehe B'Jean come here! I wanna kiss I wanna cuddle Where's doggy? Doggy come here! Paper Look! That's paper Let's talk Let's whistle I wanna good kiss! Thank you"

$\mathcal{M}$y holiday card for 2004, featuring Blanche, Daisy, Kaylee, and Cosmo (dear sweet Holly had died during the year of old age), was accompanied by the usual Christmas letter. This is Cosmo's part of that letter, her greeting to the world, compiled of her life list of words and phrases.

Cosmo learned all this language from me—or, in the case of my telephone number, from the telephone answering machine, which is in her room. She learned *woo woo woo* from the dogs. You can tell from what she has said to me what I have said to her. One member of Erin's graduate committee, Michael Covington, says that we need to call Cosmo's language Cosmish, to distinguish it from the grammatically, morphologically, syntactically, semantically, and symbolically complex English the rest of us speak. I look forward to Erin's future scientific work on how closely Cosmish resembles English.

Cosmo has a clean vocabulary, except for the word "poop," with which she is somehow obsessed. I don't allow any of my friends to use bad words in my house. My brother Branch, who lives in El Paso, thought he'd fool me by surreptitiously teaching Cosmo bad words on the answering machine. I'd arrive home, see the red light blinking, get all excited that somebody was leaving me a message, press the button, and hear: "Hello, Cosmo. Here's a new word for you: FART. Remember: FART. Good-bye." That wasn't funny. Fortunately, Cosmo did not remember the word. But just to stay safe, I turned down the volume of the answering machine for a while.

When I turned it back up, some weeks later, Cosmo learned my phone number, or most of it: "You have reached 706935." Later, without the area code, "You have reached 9354362. Telephone!" Usually she gets the numbers right. When she doesn't, she changes the subject: "You have reached 9354 . . . How are you?" or "You have reached 935. . . Good bird!" or "You have reached 935436 . . . Cosmo wanna peanut!"

Cosmo tries out her new words and phrases outside my presence. She practices. In the months when she was first learning to talk, Cosmo practiced her language early in the morning. When I stayed in bed late—past sunrise—on Saturdays and Sundays, I would listen to her talking to herself, trying out new words and doing her usual whistles, bird songs, phone rings, and household beeps, peeps, and squeaks. Finally, I would hear her call out loudly and insistently, "I'm here!" Our usual weekend morning conversation went like this:

Cosmo: "I'm here!"
BJC: "Mmmmm"
Cosmo: "I'm here!"
BJC: "Mmmmm"
Cosmo: "Here I am! I'm here!"
BJC: "Okay, I'm coming."
Cosmo: "Here are you?"
BJC: "I'm coming! I'm coming!"

When I opened the door to her room, Cosmo would declare: "Cosmo wanna poop!" Cosmo did not want to do her big morning poop inside her cage. So after I let her out, she would climb up to her playscape perch and poop from there onto the newspapers. Then she'd announce: "Cosmo poop!" Lately she has been doing her morning poop on the floor on her way into my bedroom, informing me, "Cosmo poop!"

Many African Greys won't defecate where they sleep because in the wild they don't want to reveal their roost location to predators. They excrete their urine and feces together through the cloaca, an organ sometimes referred to as the vent, which they also use for mating and laying eggs. The two-second act of mating biologists call a "cloacal kiss." *Cloaca* comes from the word *sewer* in Latin.

While I'm on this subject, I should say that Cosmo usually tells me whenever she has pooped on the floor, which is hardwood throughout the house, thank goodness. She knows that I will come clean up her droppings with a paper towel and a vinegar—no ammonia— cleanser. As I bend over to spray the cleanser on the floor, Cosmo will enthusiastically make the spray sound *whisss*, and then, referring to the towel, exclaim, "That's paper!" My sister Mary Jo once told me that I was getting old if when I bent over to pick up one thing off the floor I looked around while I was down there to see whether I could pick up another thing on the same trip. Well, yes, I do that. When I bend over to wipe the floor clean I pick up any peanut shells, dead leaves, feathers, or fur that I can grab before I have to straighten up. Sometimes I groan a teeny bit when I bend over. The other day I noticed that when I bent over to wipe up a little mess, with Cosmo riding on my left hand, Cosmo groaned.

When she's out and about Cosmo poops at regular five-minute intervals, but she never poops on me, even when I'm holding her for long periods of time. So I can't help speculating that she poops frequently on the floor for the sheer pleasure of watching me clean up after her.

In December of 2004, Cosmo still called me "B'-Jean," but now she pronounces my name correctly and says "Betty Jean." She learned my name one morning when I was about to step into the shower and she was saying, "Time for shower and a peanut for Cosmo." Cosmo loves her misting and requests it every day as soon as I have finished eating my breakfast. That morning I said, "No, it's time for shower for Betty Jean!" She repeated: "Time for shower for B'Jean!" "Time for shower for B'Jean!" She caught on immediately that I was "B'Jean." And she caught on that my shower from the faucet meant the same to me as her shower from the misting bottle meant to her. It meant getting soaked in water, whether one had a little body with lots of feathers or a big body with no feathers.

Cosmo then used my name in other contexts: "B' Jean, come here!" "B'Jean wanna kiss?" "Telephone for B'Jean!" She had already learned that the dogs had names, and that she could call them by name and get their attention, so she used my name often thereafter to get my attention. I began referring to myself in third person and enunciating the consonants of my name more carefully, as in "Betty Jean wanna go to kitchen." Soon Cosmo was saying, "Time for shower for Betty Jean"—though never "Time for shower and a peanut for Betty Jean."

What is remarkable, I think, is not her learning my

name but her learning that everything in her world has a name, a name which I can tell her and which she can employ to get what she wants. What a conceptual leap for a bird! I suspect she perceives an advantage to knowing the words for things in her immediate environment, things she can request, even though she doesn't say the words immediately, and may not ever say them.

So how has Cosmo learned to talk so well? I imagine that most parrots pick up language from their home environment, from family members speaking with each other. They can eavesdrop on conversations, phone calls, arguments, shouts and laughs, and intimate exchanges, and repeat or employ what they like. But I am the only human in my household. So I speak directly to Cosmo, and she responds directly to me. Leaning forward and tilting her head so that she can see me clearly with one eye, she leads me to believe that everything I say to her is fascinating. When I am home Cosmo and I talk constantly.

Long ago, when I was in the early stages of learning foreign languages, I had difficulty understanding native speakers when they conversed rapidly and colloquially. But I could understand them when they spoke directly to me and used the vocabulary I had been acquiring in my courses. Then I felt power—even joy—in my new ability to communicate my ideas to people who didn't speak English. When I could finally chat without translating in my head, I knew that I could make myself at home in the foreign language. This is what Cosmo has accomplished with English. She has made herself at home in English.

So like foreign language teachers I use a simplified syntax and limited vocabulary with Cosmo, I look at her when I speak, and I consistently use the same words and phrases. For example, I always say, "Cosmo wanna go in a car?" and never vary the question with synonyms. I don't say "Cosmo wanna ride?" or "Would you like to go for a drive in the automobile?" I say "peanut" for all kinds of nuts: peanuts, walnuts, pecans, pistachios, and—by far the best, in her opinion—cashews. I wish she'd never tasted cashews, because now she will sometimes refuse the dry-roasted unsalted peanuts I give her. She became acquainted with cashews when she spent a weekend Margaret and Wyatt, who buy cashews for themselves and share them with her.

I used to say "Cosmo room" instead of "Cosmo's room" and "Betty Jean bedroom" instead of "Betty Jean's bedroom," but I must have slipped from time to time and used the possessive, for lately I've heard Cosmo say, "Let's go to Betty Jean's bedroom."

My friends no longer say that Cosmo sounds like me, and she really does, but rather that I sound like Cosmo. I'm probably using a simplified syntax, limited vocabulary, and Cosmo's intonation when talking with them now. "Helloooo. How are YOU?" "Wanna come to dinner?"

Cosmo has been able to learn new vocabulary quickly and to expand her communication with a relatively few basic concepts. Cosmo can use these phrases to say what she wants, to request things, to ask and answer basic questions, and to get information.

Step up. Go up.
No
Good
Bad
Cosmo wanna _____ (peanut, kiss, go to bed, go to kitchen)
Cosmo wanna _____?

Hafta _____ (Betty Jean hafta go to work)
Where
Where? (Where are you?)
Here
I love you
What's that? That's _____ (squirrel, paper, peanut, clothes for Betty Jean)
Okay
Okay?
Don't
Gonna _____ (go in a car, leave, go to work)
For (clothes for Betty Jean, water for Cosmo's cage, telephone for bird)
Time for _____
Wow
With
And
More

Cosmo must have deduced from my speech that a particular intonation indicates a question that requires an answer. The first instance of her asking me a question was her use of "okay" as a question: "Cosmo wanna peanut, okay?" Most likely she learned it from my saying "Okay" in response to her statement "Cosmo wanna peanut." I don't know how she learned "What's that?" but she uses it whenever she encounters something new.

Cosmo and I use "okay" to consent to a request made by the other, and "okay?" to ask for consent. For example, if Cosmo has done something bad, like biting me, and I have put her "back in cage," which she pronounces *caije*, we may have this conversation:

> COSMO: "Cosmo wanna go up, okay?
> BJC: "No, Cosmo is a bad bird. Cosmo stay in cage."
> COSMO: "Cosmo be a good bird, okay?"
> BJC: "Cosmo be a good bird. Stay in cage."

COSMO: "Cosmo wanna be a good bird, okay?"
BJC: "Cosmo stay in cage."
COSMO: "Cosmo don't bite, okay?"
BJC: "Okay. Cosmo go up."

And I open the cage door to let her out. I'm not much of a disciplinarian.

Long before Cosmo could talk, I would use the term "wanna" with her. Holding her on my left hand, I would ask her, "Cosmo wanna peanut?" and then would give her a peanut; "Cosmo wanna kiss?" and would kiss her lightly on her surprisingly warm beak; "Cosmo wanna go to kitchen?" and would take her to the kitchen, her favorite room in the house. Although she could do nothing more than whistle, she was learning that the sounds that I, a human, made had meanings.

Cosmo and I use "gonna" to express a future event. "We're gonna have company!" "We're gonna go in a car!" Cosmo combines "wanna" and gonna" to ask, "Where wanna gonna go?" Because the formulation of the question is logical, I don't correct her.

Cosmo has also learned to use "and" and "with," as in "Cosmo and Betty Jean wanna whistle?" and "Cosmo stay home with doggies" and "Cosmo go to work with Betty Jean?"

Since she usually has the run of the house when I'm home, I often need to inquire, "Cosmo, where are you?" Unless she's doing something particularly naughty that she doesn't want me to notice, she will whistle or respond "I'm here!" and I can locate her. When I find her I'll say, "There you are!" When the situation is reversed and Cosmo wants to locate me, she'll call out "Here are you?" This is a mistake that shows she's thinking: She has turned "I'm here" into the question "Here are you?" When she finds me she'll say, with a lilt that sounds just

43

like mine, "There you are!" My heart melts when I arrive home after a long day, open the squeaky door from the garage, and hear Cosmo say, "There you are!"

Cosmo correctly uses the pronouns *you* and *I*. She learned you and I by generalizing from "I love you," and listening to me speak in the first person to her. When she was learning to talk she would say, in the right situation, "I love you" and "Cosmo wanna kiss!" This might be when I was holding her, or it might be when she was sitting serenely atop her cage behind me in my study while I worked at the computer. Later, "Betty Jean wanna kiss?" More recently, "I wanna kiss" and "Do you wanna kiss?" followed by a long, drawn-out, super-fancy, unrepeatable "*smooooooooch*." After the *smooch*, she often says, "Wow! That's good kiss!"

At first, "kiss" meant my touching her head gently with my lips and making a very soft smooch. That was before she could talk. Pretty soon I was kissing her beak with a smooch. Then I was kissing her at a distance of one inch through her cage bars before I left the house in the morning: "*Smooch*." Then she was throwing me a kiss from inside her cage: "*Smoooch*." Eventually, Cosmo would say, "Cosmo and Betty Jean wanna kiss?" We developed a game of long-distance kiss. Whoever could *smooch* at long distance for the most seconds won. I'd do "*Smooooch!*" She always won: "*Smoooooooooooch!* Wow!"

Cosmo usually uses the pronoun *we* appropriately, as in "We're gonna go to kitchen," "We're gonna go in a car!" and "We're gonna have company!" But sometimes she'll say, "We're gonna go for a walk," and then I don't know whether she is including herself in "we" to be funny—since she often says, "Cosmo wanna go for a walk! Nooooo. Cosmo is a bird!"—or she doesn't comprehend fully the concept of first person plural.

Cosmo picked up "No!" right away. When I say it to her, in a louder-than-normal voice, she immediately turns around and stops what she's doing, for a moment. The word may not have given her a conscience, by our standards, but it has given her a fair idea of what is or is not permissible behavior in my house. If she's doing something out of my sight that she knows is wrong, like making sawdust of a wood molding or taking a pen apart, I'll hear her mutter softly to herself, "No, no, no, bad bird!" Then I know I'd better hurry to the scene of her crime. If she hears me coming down the hall towards her, she'll quickly stop her activity and scurry off. And I may fail to catch her if she scurries at top speed—in her adorable parrot-toed gait—under her cage or under my bed.

Cosmo also uses "No!" with the dogs. One day, as she was waddling down the hall toward the kitchen, Blanche approached her and sniffed her rear end, as was Blanche's customary means of getting acquainted with dogs. Cosmo turned around sharply and scolded, "No, no, no!" Blanche retreated quickly, possibly embarrassed. I dog-sat Branch and Siobhan's lively puppy Sally one weekend, and when the puppy jumped up and down trying to snag my sleeve with her sharp incisors, Cosmo reprimanded her: "No, no, bad dog!" Cosmo acts as if she were assistant manager of the household. If I'm reading in her room and my little dog Mary leaps onto my lap, Cosmo will look down from her perch atop her cage and say: "No, no, no! Mary, move!"

Cosmo had more difficulty grasping the concept of "Don't." She probably learned the word from my saying, "Ow! Don't bite!" She also learned "Ow!" from the same situation. But she didn't use the word "don't" as a negative in a declarative sentence until she'd been speaking for a year or so. Then one morning she said, "Cosmo don't wanna go to kitchen." She regularly promises, "Cosmo don't bite, okay?" as if the default mode were "Cosmo bite!" A few weeks ago she said, after lunging at me as if to bite, "Cosmo don't wanna be a good bird."

In her first year of speaking, Cosmo made lots of sounds I couldn't understand, among them "*Whaaaaay.*" One day when she said "*Whaaaaay,*" I asked her, "Cosmo, what's that?" Cosmo said, "That's water!" Oh, my! She was translating into English for me the sound of the water coming out of the faucet where I refilled her dish.

Lately, Cosmo has been trying to say the word desk, as in "Cosmo wanna go to Betty Jean's desk." I hadn't tried to teach her the word. Actually, I tried to teach her "Betty Jean's study," which she never learned to say. I must have said "desk" only once or twice before she tried to say the word to refer to the table where my computer rests. But she could not say the word perfectly. She said, "sesk"—"Cosmo wanna go to Betty Jean's sesk." I heard her practicing the word: "Sesk . . . Betty Jean's sesk . . . Betty Jean's desk . . . desk . . . Cosmo wanna go to Betty Jean's desk." Or, on occasion, still, "Cosmo wanna go to Betty's desk." Even "Cosmo wanna go to Betty Jean's deck."

Although Cosmo usually speaks clearly and intelligently, sometimes she does not, and sometimes she makes mistakes. She may begin a sentence and fail to finish it, or say a word unintelligibly, or start a thought and end with a different thought—perhaps changing the subject to distract me from her mistake. Examples: "Cosmo wanna . . . how are you?" "Doggies go for a . . . We're gonna have company!" "Cosmo is whatta bird . . . feathers." When I know what she's trying to say, I say it back to her. When I don't know, I say, "What?" But then she may say "What?" back to me and we're trapped in a round of *what*. Kind of like "Who's on first?"

> COSMO: "Cosmo wanna go to kitch . . .
> BJC: "What?"
> COSMO: What?"
> BJC: Cosmo wanna go to kitchen?
> COSMO: "What?"

For years Cosmo has enjoyed the game of "What's that?" She will hear a chirp in the woods and ask, "What's that?" If I don't reply immediately she will answer her own question: "That's birdy." When she mimics the dogs, I get it immediately:

> COSMO: "*Woo woo woo*. What's that?"
> BJC: "That's doggy!"
> COSMO: "That's doggy bark!"

And when I'm dressing, I can tell what she's looking at.

> COSMO: "What's that?"
> BJC: "That's clothes."
> COSMO: "That's clothes for Betty Jean!"

Yet I don't always know whether she's asking about something she's hearing or something she's seeing. So we have conversations like the following:
> COSMO: "What's that?"
> BJC: "What?"
> COSMO: "What?"

By asking "What's that?" Cosmo learned the names for "clothes," "television," which took her some time to pronounce right, "bark," and a host of other things. She asks, "What's that?" for almost anything she finds intriguing for which she doesn't have a name. When I play a new CD, she asks, "What's that?" I answer only,

"Music." Perhaps she thinks I can't discriminate between Il Divo and Dvořák.

I repeat Cosmo's utterances back to her often, so that she will retain good pronunciation. If I don't, she gets careless. And if I don't keep using her vocabulary, she forgets words. She once knew the word apple, but she doesn't use it anymore, even when I do. She says "Cosmo wanna grape," but she no longer knows what a grape is. We don't have grapes in the winter.

Friends have asked me why I don't teach Cosmo to say, "I'm a Democrat." I reply that I don't want her to learn any words she can't comprehend and use effectively. That's why I don't speak to her in Spanish, which is my second language. When I take a dirt nap in a few years—I mean, go to heaven—and Cosmo goes to live with another family, I don't want her to have a vocabulary that is not functional. Since African Greys ordinarily live fifty years, I want Cosmo to be able converse with everybody she meets. I also want her to be a nice bird whom her future companions will love.

Cosmo's ability to tell me what she wants has given her great self-confidence. Cosmo no-----t only can request things for herself but can also tell me what to do. She reminds me when it's time for me to take a shower, when it's time for us to go to the kitchen, when it's time for me to put seed out for the squirrels, when it's time for the dogs to go for a walk, when it's time for her to go to bed. She knows our routine. She chastises the dogs when appropriate. She says "Please," to reinforce her demands. She tells me what she needs in her cage: "Cosmo wanna peanut for cage!" "More water for cage!" Or "No more water in cage." She may be exhibiting parental behavior, since in the wild African Greys teach their chicks what to eat, where to go, how to act, and what time to do things. I used to tell Cosmo when it's time to go to the kitchen; now she tells me. She's no longer a chick.

Cosmo knows what she likes and what she dislikes. One early morning Cosmo had asked me, "Where gonna go?" I said, "Betty Jean gonna go in a car." Cosmo responded, "Nooooo!" And she knows where she wants to go. She knows all the rooms of the house and what they offer. If I won't give her a ride on my hand to her destination, she will walk. She especially likes my bathroom, which until recently she called "shower for Betty Jean room." Now she has somehow learned the word bathroom. I had avoided using the word out of fear that she would tell company that I was in the bathroom. But one day, to my astonishment, she said, "Cosmo wanna go to bathroom"—and she did not mean that she wanted to poop. She loves to go to my bathroom, where she can open drawers and extract emery boards, bottles, jars, tubes, and lipsticks.

All of this shows that Cosmo has an active mental life. She thinks. For most people, parrots are simply mimics, clever mimics perhaps, but not thinkers. Without any malice whatsoever, some parrot keepers may neglect their pet bird in ignorance of the bird's feelings and the bird's need for intellectual stimulation. They may keep the bird confined to the cage, for the sake of convenience. Or they may buy CDs that play certain phrases over and over to teach the bird to "talk," phrases such as "Parrot wanna cracker." That's not talking. For the life of me I can't understand why folks find entertaining a bird's utterance of a phrase the bird doesn't understand. The repetition of something nonsensical can drive a smart parrot to feather-pluck, just as the repeated playing of "Jingle Bells" can drive me to bat my head against the wall.

By the way, the phrase "Polly wanna cracker" may have originated in Andrew Jackson's presidency. President Jackson had a parrot named Poll, who, according to legend, had to be removed from the president's funeral ceremony because of his foul utterances. I like the fact that the parrot attended the funeral.

Cosmo is obviously capable of mimicry. Witness her imitation of the sounds of the house, the sounds of the woods, and the sounds of the street. But the cliché that parrots can only mimic, that they have no mental life, serves as a pre-Darwinian justification for our not respecting them. It leads to their abuse.

I learned about the intelligence of African Greys from Irene Pepperberg's research and from Irene herself. At my invitation, Irene gave a lecture on Alex's cognitive achievements at the University of Georgia, where she filled a large hall to standing room only and left behind four hundred fans, who continue to alert me whenever she is on television or on the radio or in the *New York Times*. The morning that *NPR* announced its upcoming "Fresh Air" interview with Irene upon the publication of her book *Alex and Me*, I received over ten emails and phone calls telling me to turn on WUGA-FM at noon. I did. And I learned that Alex, when he misbehaved, apologized by saying, "I'm sorry." Cosmo just says, cheerfully, "Cosmo bad bird. Back in cage." Cosmo is not remorseful, nor does she get her feelings hurt when scolded—unlike my sensitive dogs. She remains chipper—chirping, whistling, talking, ringing the phone, and laughing—even after being locked in her cage.

Inspired by Irene's success in teaching Alex to name colors and shapes and to count, I decided to teach Cosmo to count to three. I say "One kiss. *Smooch*. That's one kiss." And I hold up one finger. Then I say, "Two kiss. *Smooch smooch*. That's two kiss." And I hold up two fingers. Then I say, "Three kiss. *Smooch smooch smooch*. That's three kiss." And I hold up three fingers. Cosmo watches me intently, and then says, "*Smooch*. That's one kiss." She also says, "Three kiss. *Smooch smooch smooch*. That's three kiss." But she doesn't always get "three" right. Occasionally, she'll say, "Three kiss. *Smooch smooch smooch smooch*. That's three kiss." And I promptly say, "That's four kiss!" Cosmo doesn't do "two."

In order to teach Cosmo that numbers are abstract, that they refer not just to kisses, I have begun saying "*Woo woo woo*! That's three bark." "*Woo woo*! That's two bark." "*Woo*! That's one bark." She pays attention—that is, she doesn't climb off her perch to go elsewhere.

Sometimes I wish I hadn't started this lesson, because I feel obliged to concentrate on what Cosmo says whenever she starts practicing "one," "two," and "three." And she practices a lot. She appears especially interested in the difference between one and three.

I tried to teach Cosmo to distinguish between red feathers and gray feathers. Cosmo had already learned the word "feather," and she often proclaims, "Cosmo has feathers! Cosmo is a bird!" But she could not, or would not, say, "red feather" or "gray feather." She would simply grab the feather with her beak and fling it away, gleefully. I decided that my teaching method for visual cues may have been unsuited to my purposes.

Irene had modified the "model-rival" method, created by German animal behaviorist Dietmar Todt, to teach Alex and the other Greys in her laboratory. The teaching method is based on the presumed desire of parrots, and other animals, to compete for primacy in their

51

group. With Alex watching, Irene would teach a lab assistant what she wanted Alex to learn—a label for a piece of pasta, a cube, etcetera. When the lab assistant answered correctly, Irene would reward her with the piece of pasta or the cube or whatever. Soon Alex would compete with the lab assistant to give the correct answers, and Alex would receive the reward, whatever he had identified. Irene was not always the trainer, and the assistant was not always the pupil, so Alex learned that he could join in the game and play the role of either trainer or assistant. Irene reported one such session in *The Alex Studies* (page 206), in which "peg wood" is a clothes pin, which is called "clothes peg" in England:

K [Katherine]: OK, Alex, let's start. What's this? (Holds up clothes pin.)
A [Alex]: Peg wood.
I [Irene]: (Sits facing wall, observing neither A nor K): That's "peg wood."
K: That's right—here's the peg wood, Alex. You're a good boy. (Hands over the clothes pin.)
A: (Takes clothes pin, but drops it immediately): Want cork.
K: OK, here's cork.
(A plays with the cork for about one minute.)
K: Enough, Alex. Gimme cork (holds out her hand; Alex relinquishes cork). What's this, what shape? (Holds up a red, triangular piece of wood.)
A. Cor-er wood.
I: I think he said, "corner wood."
K: (Briefly turns away, then reestablishes eye contact with parrot): Alex, what shape? Talk clearly!!
A: Three-corner wood.
I: "Three-corner wood."
K: You're right—that shape is three-corner wood. (Hands wood to parrot.)
(A takes wood, chews off one of the corners, drops it.)

A: Wanna nut. (K gives him a nut, which he eats.)
K: Look, what's this? (Holds up a piece of grey rawhide.)
A: Wanna nut.
K: No nuts . . . first tell me, what's this?
A: Grey hi'.
I: "Grey hide."
K: Good parrot . . . here's the grey hide.
A: (Refuses to take the hide): Wanna nut!

Alex demonstrated not only high intelligence but also wit and willfulness, as Irene chronicles in *Alex and Me*.

I do not have another human at home with whom Cosmo can compete. Cosmo competes with the dogs for my attention, very successfully, but she views the dogs as inferior to herself, perhaps because they cannot talk. And though I love my dogs passionately—now reduced in number to two—Kaylee and Mary—I must admit that they don't demand the intellectual attention that Cosmo does. They do demand cuddling, like Cosmo. Sort of like Cosmo.

Actually, come to think of it, I do have humans with whom Cosmo competes: my dinner guests. Whenever I have folks to dinner, we usually sit first in the living room, just out of Cosmo's sight, where we have wine and hors d'oeuvres and lively conversation. When the guests laugh, Cosmo listens attentively from her cage in the dining room and laughs, too, or at least makes the sound of laughter. She has two different laughs: an out-loud laugh, similar to my out-loud laugh but more raucous, which I represent as *hahaha*; and a giggle, similar to my giggle, which I represent as *hehehe*. Soon after the guests' arrival she will whistle to get everybody's attention, and then tell her jokes and laugh gaily when the guests laugh. Here is a short example of Cosmo's typical behavior with guests:

[Guests arrive, sit in living room. Cosmo is quiet for a few minutes. Then she whistles.]

> COSMO: "*Whee whew!*" [Guests laugh. Cosmo whistles a half-tune, perhaps part of "The Bridge On the River Kwai." Guests laugh again and mention Cosmo's name.]
> COSMO: "We've got company!"
> [Guests laugh, mention Cosmo's name again.]
> COSMO: "Hello! How are YOU?"
> SOMEBODY: "Hello, Cosmo."
> COSMO: "Cosmo wanna peanut" [She notices if guests are served cashews.]
> SOMEBODY: "May we give Cosmo a nut?"
> COSMO: "Cosmo wanna peanut! Wanna peanut!" [Cosmo gets her cashew. That's one reason she loves company: With company she gets cashews.]
> COSMO: "*Rrrring*. Telephone for bird! *Hahaha!*"
> [Guests laugh.]
> COSMO: "You have reached Cosmo!" *Hahaha!*
> COSMO: "Cosmo wanna peanut!"
> [Cosmo may ask to get out of her cage.]
> COSMO: "Cosmo wanna go up, okay? Cosmo be a good bird!"

If the guests continue to interact with her, Cosmo will continue to try to make them laugh. Whether she is competing with them for dominance, I don't know. But she is competing with them for attention. She does want to join the party, and she knows fun when she hears it.

If the guests turn to a different subject, like politics, Cosmo will grow quiet, perhaps uttering a "Yoohoo" or a "Hello" from time to time, perhaps talking in a low voice to herself: "Cosmo is a bird. Good bird. We've got company" or "Telephone for Cosmo. *Hehehe.*"

When the guests come into the dining room for dinner, Cosmo will cease her chatter and spend an hour or so preening contentedly. Thus we can always have good people-talk at the dinner table. Then Cosmo will ask to go up, and I'll open her cage door. If I'm not looking, however, she'll climb down to the floor, walk around, and bite somebody's foot. She especially likes women's toes if the toenails are painted. So everybody will be animatedly discussing something, like a presidential election, and suddenly somebody will let out a shriek. I'll apologize profusely and scramble around on the floor to get Cosmo back into her cage. I'll yell at her, "Cosmo is a bad bird! Go back in cage! Don't bite!" She'll mutter, "Cosmo go back in cage."

If guests stay too long, Cosmo will announce, "Time to go to bed!" for which I'm grateful. Cosmo will keep making her point till the guests get up from the table, and then she will say, sweetly, "Good-bye." Often she will accompany the dogs and me to the door to bid our guests farewell. There she is, less than a foot high, mingling self-assuredly with six or seven grown-up humans and two fairly grown-up dogs and saying, like any gracious hostess, "Good-bye."

To Cosmo, "go to bed" means first going into "Betty Jean's bedroom," then preening for a half hour or so, then enjoying a cuddle, and lastly being taken into her roost cage to sleep.

There is no scarcity of information about keeping African Greys as pets. I am indebted not only to Irene Pepperberg for teaching me about Greys' cognitive ability and to *Bird Talk* magazine for teaching me about parrots in general, but also to Mattie Sue Athan and Dianalee Deter, authors of *The African Grey Parrot Hand-*

book, for teaching me about Greys' bodies, and to Maggie Wright, author of *African Grey Parrots* and editor of The Grey Play Roundtable, which devoted its last issue to Alex, for teaching me about Greys' behavior patterns and their relationships with their people.

I am indebted to Cosmo for teaching me that when she ruffles up her feathers to look fierce she is about to bite.

From the *Handbook* I learned about the formation of feathers. All feathers begin as "blood feathers," growing from tiny follicles in the outer layer of the bird's skin in a tapered spike that contains the blood supply. As the spike grows, the feather will emerge, and the sheath that formed the spike will dry up and flake off, turning into dander. If the bird breaks the blood feather accidentally, the bird can bleed profusely and may need to have the vet extract the feather.

Birds preen themselves to remove the sheath from the feathers and to keep them in good condition. With their beak they extract oil from the uropygial gland, or preen gland, by their tail and coat their feathers with it, waterproofing them. Without an avian mate to take care of spots they can't reach with their beaks, pet parrots like for us humans gently to caress their heads and necks.

If African Greys have a stressful environment, or if they lack intellectual and emotional stimulation, or if they are unloved, they show their unhappiness by plucking their feathers out. That is one aspect of their high intelligence. To stay in good health, Greys need fun in their lives, brain work, attention from their human companions, lots of things to do and see from within their cage, and a few hours outside their cage, every day. They also need eight hours of full-spectrum lighting and at least ten hours of continuous nighttime sleep.

African Greys, like many species of parrots that get

a daily drenching in the rain forest, need regular misting to keep the powder they exude from causing health
problems. I am amazed by Cosmo's knowing that her
misting, my shower, and her bath in the dogs' large
water dish in the laundry room are all the same thing,
"shower," which is desirable. When she takes her bird-
bath, she flings herself into the dish, gets all wet, flaps
her wings vigorously, and then climbs out, saying "Wow!
Good shower!"

I learned from the *Handbook* that a bird cannot
catch a human cold. I had wondered about that when I
arrived home after a trip to hear Cosmo making the
sound of a sneeze. But apparently that was all she was
doing: making the sound of a sneeze. She was mimicking
the sneeze of the puppy/parrot-sitter, who must have
had a cold. I got one two days later.

Have you ever heard the remark, "Something stuck
in his craw"? Craw is another word for a bird's crop, an
expandable muscular pouch that is part of the bird's
esophagus. The bird stores food there temporarily prior
to digesting it. For example, if I give Cosmo fresh
peanuts, which she eats in a hurry before I take them
away, she'll store them in her crop. One evening after
Cosmo had said, "I love you," I lifted her up to my lips for
a kiss. I'm used to her peanut breath. On this occasion
she bobbed her head up and down and deposited a piece
of peanut in my mouth. "Thank you," I said. I found out
later that this was mating behavior—"the sign of true
love," according to Athan and Deter—which I should not
encourage. I don't want Cosmo—now sexually mature—
to lay an egg in the cage. What would I do with her egg?
I'm not sure I'd feel right about eating it.

African Greys are monogamous in the wild. That's

why I'm Cosmo's mate at home. Her calls to me of "I'm here!" and "Where are you?" function like contact calls to a mate to determine the mate's location.

Parrots, like all birds, make their sounds by whistling. Their vocal organ is not the larynx but the syrinx, a bony structure at the base of the trachea, through which air flows into and out of the lungs. The syrinx is the bird's songbox. When air flows through the syrinx, the bird tightens the syrinx muscles to make the membrane vibrate and produce sound, controlling the pitch and the volume by controlling the force of exhaling. In *The Alex Studies* Irene Pepperberg explains how African Greys can mimic the human voice and make their variety of other sounds: They use not only the syrinx but also the larynx, an avian larynx which modifies the sound produced by the syrinx, instead of producing sound itself, the tongue, the glottis, the beak, and probably even the esophagus.

A parrot's beak, like any other bird's beak, continues to grow during the parrot's lifetime. The part of the beak closest to the parrot's head has a blood supply, as well as nerve endings, and that is why it's warm. The sharp end of the beak does not have a blood supply, and it can be filed down by the vet if necessary. Parrots have strong hooked beaks, which are capable of cracking hard nuts in the wild and taking the staples out of magazines in the home. They need access to materials they can bite safely, like wooden toys, ropes, peanuts, and—Cosmo thinks—plastic waste paper baskets, emery boards, and baseboards, to keep their beaks in good shape. I provide Cosmo with a cement perch in each of her cages for the health of her beak and her feet.

Most parrots—and owls and woodpeckers—have zygodactyl feet, with the second and third toes projecting forward and the first and fourth toes projecting backward. Zygodactyl feet are useful for climbing trees, or cages, and for eating. Cosmo uses her feet as hands to pick up her food and hold it while eating. One day I noticed that her right foot had turned reddish, and I worried about it until I realized that she had been eating a sweet red pepper and holding it with her right foot. Her dexterity gives her the ability to take the tops off lipsticks, eyeliners, pens, highlighters, and anything else that she can hold with one foot and control with her beak. I'm trying to teach her to drink juice out of a measuring cup she can lift with her foot, but I'm not having any success. Cosmo would prefer to drink juice out of my glass.

A parrot should have several perches of different diameters in her cage in order not to get arthritis from standing too long in the same position. Parrots stand all day and all night, and they need to keep their feet flexible. At night, or in the daytime when she's dozing, Cosmo stands on one foot and tucks the other one up under her feathers. Cosmo's veterinary checkups include a nail trim, a beak trim, and a feather trim. Hope Animal Clinic is both her doctor's office and her beauty shop.

Bird Talk carries articles about the many varieties of parrots and about their different temperaments, their food preferences and food sensitivities, their tendency to feather-pluck when bored or distressed, and their potential for speaking, as well as their vulnerability to Teflon poisoning and their need for good indoor air quality. Overheated Teflon emits fumes that are toxic to birds. It was from *Bird Talk* that I found out that African Greys don't talk until they are a year old, that they usually bond with one person, that they mature sexually at approximately six years old, and that they have the temperament of a two-year-old child. I found out that their fragile systems cannot tolerate alcohol, avocado, caffeine, chocolate, grease, salt, ammonia, scented candles, and cigarette smoke. No margaritas with guacamole and chips for Cosmo. No séances either.

Nevertheless, parrots enjoy many of the wholesome fruits, vegetables, and nuts that we humans eat. Cosmo eats nuts of all kinds, pasta, snow peas, snap peas, English peas, lima beans, corn, okra, zucchini, crooked neck squash, acorn squash, sweet potato, carrots, red peppers, bell peppers, tomatoes, grapes, pears, apples, oranges, papaya, strawberries, raspberries, blueberries, and cherries. She also regularly eats fruit-flavored pellets for parrots and chili-flavored pellets for parrots

Many parrot owners argue—convincingly to me— that clipping a parrot's flight feathers is a good thing to do, for it prevents the parrot from flying into a ceiling fan, against a window, or through a door open to the outside. Yet their claim does have its opposition. The journal *Bio-Medicine* carried an article on May 6, 2008, asserting that "Thousands of pet parrots are developing psychological problems as a direct result from having their God-given right to fly stripped away from them from unknowing pet owners." The issue merits some pondering, for even though some of us less God-fearing pet owners may question the concept of God-given avian rights, none of us wants to cause suffering. However, I wonder what proof the writer has that psychological problems result directly from the feather clipping. I have concluded that psychological harm may be produced by a variety of conditions, including extended confinement. If I let Cosmo fly freely through my house, I would not give her as much freedom from her cage as I presently do. I like for her to have free run of my house whenever

I'm home, and so does she. If Cosmo is brooding about her inability to fly, I certainly don't detect it. I detect mostly her joyful independence.

The first time the vet wrapped a towel around Cosmo to subdue her for a feather trim, Cosmo looked up at me and said pitifully, "Cosmo wanna be a good bird!" Since then, all I have to do to get Cosmo to step up on my hand is to ask, "Cosmo wanna towel?" When I bring out the towel, she says, "That's towel!" and promptly hops on my hand.

African Grey Parrots do not require regular shots from the vet, as do dogs and cats, nor do they get smelly, as do ferrets, hamsters, gerbils, mice, guinea pigs, and rabbits. They need not be taken outside on a leash. They do not screech like Amazons, Macaws, and Cockatoos, and their poop is less voluminous than that of those larger parrots. They are reputed to be among the most intelligent birds in the world, perhaps the most talkative, and the only species capable of imitating almost exactly the human voice—incredibly, since birds do not have vocal chords. At a dinner party one evening, my friend Hugh said that Cosmo sounded like she could be a female cousin of mine.

Although Cosmo usually speaks in my voice, she does use other voices when she is speaking to other people. When she was barely a year old, I came home one day after Greg had been painting my hallway. Greg, who has a fondness for parrots, had spent the day talking with Cosmo while he worked. I walked in the door, and Cosmo said, in Greg's low voice, "Hello. How are you?" That was her first venture into other voices. Now, whenever I have men over Cosmo tries out her man's voice.

One might think that African Greys would make

perfect pets. But watch out. Charming as they can be—
and Cosmo is truly charming, except when she bites—
African Greys are very high-maintenance animals.
Because of their extraordinary intelligence, Greys need
much attention from their human families. They need
verbal and physical interaction with people, intellectual
stimulation from their environment, time outside the
cage to walk around and get exercise, an assortment of
foods, stuff to chew up and make sawdust from, and toys.
Greys are not for everyone.

Cosmo has my attention whenever I'm home, unless
I have company, in which case she has their attention
during cocktail hour when she wants it. She also has intellectual stimulation when I'm not home. In the mornings, she watches the squirrels and birds coming to the
birdfeeder on the deck, which the dogs occasionally
chase. She watches the dogs, one of whom naps on the
sofa in her room. She listens to the sounds of the woods.

And she talks to the dogs: "Doggies, come here," or
"Do you wanna go for a walk?" which she says just when
I want to relax after dinner. Then I have to leash up the
dogs and take them for a walk.

Cosmo gets plenty of freedom from her cage, and she
takes herself wherever she wants to go in the house. As
she walks down the hall she says to herself, or sometimes to me, "Cosmo wanna go to Betty Jean's bedroom,"
where she can chase Kaylee out from under the bed. Or
"Cosmo wanna go to Cosmo room," where she can chew
the telephone cord. She enjoys tearing apart catalogues
and newspapers. "That's paper!" She plays with toys inside her cage, but she prefers destroying cabinet doors,
wooden trim, and baseboards outside her cage.

All the baseboards show her bite marks. When I am
gone, the prospective new owner of my house will in-

quire of the realtor, "What happened here?"

Cosmo has stepped on my computer keyboard and left her mark on my documents. She has shredded a glasses case, removed the beads from a pair of moccasins, given a pinking-sheared look to the soles of my tennis shoes, chewed the corner of a comforter until the down escaped and filled the air of my bedroom, destroyed every highlighter and pen she could get her claws on, and removed the top of my lipstick and covered her beak with "Iced Amethyst." That's the short list.

And she bites. The other night she called, "Betty Jean, come here! Betty Jean wanna kiss a beak?" What a dear bird, I thought. I went over to kiss her, and she bit me!

> BJC: "Ow! That hurt! Cosmo is a bad, bad, bad bird! Cosmo go back in cage!"
> COSMO: "Cosmo is bad bird."
> [I lock Cosmo up in her cage and leave the room. One minute passes.]
> COSMO: "Cosmo wanna be a good bird? Cosmo go up? Cosmo don't bite, okay?"
> BJC: "Okay."

Her bites don't draw blood, but they do leave black and blue spots. I had to teach class the next day with a big bite mark on my upper lip. I didn't explain it. Maybe my students thought I was an interesting person. Cosmo has a short attention span, so I don't punish her for long. She won't remember what she has done to deserve punishment.

Anyway, my point is that African Greys are not perfect. Cosmo is not perfect. She bites. But then, I'm not perfect either. Most of the time when she says "Cosmo wanna kiss on a beak. Come here, please," she gives me a nice kiss. Sometimes a long kiss. Smoooooch. And I feel a surge of affection for her.

I tell you: You haven't lived till you've been kissed by an affectionate parrot with a little black tongue.

3. Telephone for Bird!

COSMO: "*Rrrring.............*"
COSMO: "Telephone! Telephone for Bird!"
BJC: "*Hahahahahahaha!*"
COSMO: "*Hahahahahahahahaha!*"
BJC: "*Hahahahahahahahaha!*"
COSMO: "*Hahahahahahaha!*"

"*B*ird," Cosmo said very quietly while perched on the playscape of the bedroom cage. She spoke the word several times, midst an assortment of whistles, chirps, squeaks, and beeps. After a couple of seconds, I realized what she was trying to say. She had extracted the word bird from my repeated praise "Cosmo is a good bird." Cosmo, having just celebrated her first birthday, already knew she was "Cosmo," and she uttered her name frequently.

I leapt out of my chair and said, "Yes, Cosmo is a bird!" Soon she too was saying, "Cosmo is a bird!" and "Cosmo is a good bird!" And, of course, "Cosmo is a good good good good good bird!"

In the first year of her life, in her pre-talking stage, Cosmo had listened to me whisper sweet somethings in her ear in my softest voice. Several times a day I would hold her on my hand or on my lap and say, "Hello," "I love you," "Cosmo wanna kiss?" and "Cosmo is a good bird." Cosmo learned fast those first few months after she began to talk. I can't remember the order in which she said new things, but I can remember that she called the dogs each by her right name, more or less, though with imperfect pronunciation, such as "Blash"—meaning

65

Blanche. Distinguishing the dogs from each other must not have been easy, because American Eskimo dogs look a lot alike—not to me, but to many of my human friends. These days when my youngest dog Mary goes out on the deck to bark at people or dogs or cats or squirrels or the occasional deer in the woods, Cosmo calls loudly, "Mary! Come here!" Cosmo knows the difference between Mary's bark and Kaylee's.

Mary is the newest canine member of the family, and Cosmo learned her name right away. She had already learned Kaylee's name, but after Mary's arrival she started calling Kaylee "Kary." She made the names rhyme with each other.

Since I refer to the dogs as both "dogs" and "doggies," Cosmo learned that dogs were also doggies. She'd call them to her cage, "Doggies, come here!" to get them to come to her room when I was leaving the house. One day I got home from work to hear Cosmo say, "Cosmo is a birdy!" I had never used that diminutive for bird, nor had anybody in my house to my knowledge. Now she regularly says, "Cosmo is a birdy!" And when she hears a bird chirp in the woods, she tells me either "That's a bird" or "That's a birdy." I realized with amazement that Cosmo generalized from her understanding that "dog" equaled "doggy" and "bird" equaled "birdy" when she called Kaylee "Kay." Cosmo must have thought that "Kay" equaled "Kaylee."

Not long ago I sat at my home computer, which Cosmo calls "television," responding to Cosmo's chattering with half of my mind and writing this book with the other half. Cosmo was saying such things as:

"That's television," looking at the computer screen.

"Betty Jean and Cosmo wanna whistle?"

"You have reached 9354362," or at least most of

Cosmo looking at the computer screen.

those numbers.

"How are you?" to which I would answer semi-consciously, "Fine, thank you, how are you?" and join her in a not-for-prime-time duet of "Heigh-ho, heigh-ho."

This had gone on for more than an hour when I heard Cosmo say as she looked out the picture window into the woods, "That's squirrel!" Then, "That's squirrelly!" Never in all my born days have I said the word "squirrelly." She has said it several times since then.

I have no idea how she ascertained singular and plural, but she does know the difference. Recently when I took her to the pet store for a quickie feather clip, she announced, "That's birdies," when she heard the racket the parakeets were making.

Anyway, Cosmo knew that she was a bird, not a dog and not a squirrel. She also knew what feathers were. So

I taught her that birds had feathers and dogs had fur. Early on we had conversations like this:

COSMO: "Cosmo is a birdy! Cosmo has feathers."
BJC: "Yes, bird has feathers."
COSMO: "Bird has feathers. Cosmo is a bird."
BJC: "Mary is a dog. Mary has fur."
COSMO: "Mary has fur. Mary is a doggy. *Woo woo woo woo.*"

Recently she has refused to say "fur." I don't know whether she no longer grasps the concept or is being funny, but she says, "Mary is a doggy. Mary has feathers!" I say, "No, Mary has fur." She replies, "Mary has feathers!" I say, "No! Mary has fur." Then she says, "Mary has feathers, noooo! *Hahahaha!*" This has gone on for months. Now when she says that, I say, "Mary don't have feathers!" She responds, "Mary has feathers! *Hehe.*"

Cosmo will ask me, "Betty Jean wanna kiss feathers?" and turn her side to me so that I can kiss her feathers. She smells good. Really. She'll also say, "Cosmo wanna kiss feathers," meaning that she wants a kiss on her feathers. Knowing that she has "feet," occasionally she'll lift up a foot and ask, "Betty Jean wanna kiss feet?" Kissing a parrot foot is unlike anything most humans ever experience. The four toes go everywhere across your face—one into your mouth, one into a nostril, and the other two on your cheek. I say, "Thank you."

I told Cosmo that I, Betty Jean, have clothes. So she says, "Cosmo has feathers. Betty Jean has clothes!" She pronounces the word as *cloooothes*. I can say, "Cosmo has feathers. Mary has fur. Betty Jean has . . .?" And she answers, "Clothes!"

I have tried to teach her that Betty Jean is a

"human." I say, "Cosmo is a bird. Mary is a dog. Betty Jean is a human." But whenever I say the word human, Cosmo simply shakes her head.

Cosmo recognizes herself as a bird in the mirror. She looks in the mirror when she is perched atop the cage in my bedroom and says, "That's Cosmo!" or "That's Cosmo is a good bird!" Standing on the hand-towel rack above my bathroom sink while I'm putting on my make-up, she pecks at the mirror with her beak, and proclaims, "That's Cosmo is a bird," or "That's Cosmo is whatta bird!"

But she also says, "Cosmo is a girl!" and I know she doesn't understand the word *girl*. I don't know how to explain the birds and the bees to a bird. Cosmo thinks that the word *girl* is an accolade.

Anyway, Cosmo has a clear understanding that she is a bird. She knows that the birds outside on the deck, much smaller than she, are also birds. She knows that the various bird calls she hears all day come from birds. She knows that the *rat-a-tat-tat* of a wood pecker comes from a bird. She has mastered the category of birds.

"Telephone for bird!" was Cosmo's first joke. Before she could talk, when the phone would ring, I would shout "Telephone!" for her benefit and then pick up the receiver. After she found out that I was B'Jean, she would joyfully announce "Telephone for B'Jean" at the top of her little lungs when the phone would ring or when she'd mimic the phone's *ring—"Rrrring*!" To my surprise one day, after sounding the *rrrring* from atop her cage in my bedroom, she shouted, "Telephone for bird!" I broke up laughing. Then she imitated me: "*Hahahahaha*!" And I couldn't stop laughing. There we were, a bird and a human, laughing hilariously together! What a moment. You can imagine how often thereafter she crowed "Telephone for bird! *Hahahahahaha!*"

If nobody is listening to her, she'll say quietly, "Telephone for bird. *Hehehehe.*"

I read in *Bird Talk* magazine that all kinds of large parrots laugh, or at least make the sound of laughter on appropriate occasions. Cosmo will say things to amuse herself and laugh at her own cleverness, even when she's not talking to me. From my perspective, she has a great sense of humor, or at least a sense of fun, if that is different from humor. But I can't prove it. She may just have learned that utterances of a certain type provoke laughter in people. And since she is a social animal—with a desire to be with her flock—she says things to make people laugh and stay near her. Just like us humans.

Cosmo's humor depends on an intuition of the absurd, such as the substitution of "bird" for "Betty Jean" in "Telephone for bird!" To elicit laughter, Cosmo makes all kinds of substitutions that strike her as funny—all centered upon her. For example, in place of "Doggies wanna go for a walk," she'll say "Cosmo wanna go for a walk! *Hehehe.*" In place of "Betty Jean has clothes," she'll say "Betty Jean has feathers! *Hehehe.*" In place of "Betty Jean gonna go to work," she'll say "Cosmo gonna go to work! *Hehehe.*" And in place of "Telephone for Betty Jean," she'll say "Telephone for good girl!" or "Telephone for me!" I think she enjoys imagining herself as me, a human who wears clothes, goes to work, and talks on the phone.

For Cosmo, the telephone is an infinite source for fun. Here is a sample of the telephone games that make us both laugh:

COSMO: "*Rrrring*............"
COSMO: "You have reached 9354362. Thank you. Good-bye. *Beep. Hehe.*"

COSMO: "*Rrrring*............"
COSMO: "You have reached 9354... Cosmo is a good birdy! Hahahahahaha!"

COSMO: "*Rrrring*............"
COSMO: "You have reached Betty Jean! *Hehe.*"

COSMO: "*Rrrring*............"
COSMO: "You have reached Cosmo! *Hahahahaha!*"

COSMO: "*Rrrring*............"
COSMO: "You have reached me! *Hahahaha!*"

COSMO: "*Rrrring rrrring.* Telephone! Telephone for Betty Jean. Hello (in a soft voice). How are you? Fine, thank you. Okay. Good-bye. *Beep. Hehehehe.*"

COSMO: "*Rrrring*............"
[I come out of the shower dripping wet, head towards the phone, and suddenly get suspicious.]
    BJC: "Is that Cosmo?"
    COSMO: "That's Cosmo!" *Hahahaha!*
    BJC: "*Hahahahaha!*"
    COSMO: "*Hahahaha!*"

I even tested Cosmo's timing with regard to my shower. One morning I turned on the shower, waited five seconds, and heard "*Rrrring.*" I went into the bedroom to confront Cosmo, who was perched on top of her cage with beak shut. I returned to the bathroom and again turned on the shower. Five seconds later: "*Rrrring!*" We did this three times. What fun.

I have also mistaken a real phone call for her *rrrring*, stayed in the shower, and missed the call.

I was flabbergasted to hear Cosmo refer to herself as "me." She must have generalized from "Come with me" or "Give me a kiss."

Cosmo has gotten her telephone manners from the answering machine. That's where she got my phone number, the phrase "You have reached," and the final *beep*. When she mimics my talking on the phone, she speaks softly and with my rhythms of speech. When she pretends to be the person leaving the message, she speaks in a low voice and says something unintelligible.

When I pick up the phone to make a call, Cosmo will mimic the ping of the numbers being dialed: "*Ping ping ping ping ping ping ping.*" Then she will say softly, "Hello, Joan." I call my neighbor Joan, or she calls me, every Sunday to establish that we're walking our dogs that morning. Cosmo has listened so carefully that she can repeat my side of the conversation in its entirety:

> COSMO (softly): "Hello, Joan. How are you? Fine, thank you. Wanna go for a walk? Okay. Thank you. Good-bye. *Beep. Hehe.*"

The *hehe* is Cosmo's chuckle to herself.

Cosmo appears to think that every phone call I make starts with "Hello, Joan." Whenever I pick up the phone to call somebody, she says, "Hello, Joan"—or "Hello, Jo." But I do call other people with whom I have real conversations, about life's events, politics, work, the recession, Obama. Cosmo eavesdrops, sometimes silently until she hears her name mentioned, sometimes not silently. When she hears her name mentioned she will try to interrupt. Sometimes she will pretend to be talking on the phone herself, while I'm trying to concentrate on my conversation, and will either repeat language that she has used before or mumble something that sounds like English but isn't. Then, when she wants me to get off the phone, she'll say, "Okay. Thank you. Good-bye! *Beep*." And she'll keep saying "Good-bye" till I get frustrated and end the conversation or go to another room.

I have held the receiver up to her ear to teach her to talk on the phone. She cocks her head, listens attentively to the person speaking to her, and pecks at the receiver or, occasionally, answers "Hello" in a very low voice. When I'm out of town and Cosmo is staying with Margaret and Wyatt, I call her and talk to her, but the conversation is not two-way. I also call her from my office, just for fun, and speak to her through the answering machine.

After spending her first weekend at the home of Margaret and Wyatt, Cosmo returned whistling variations on a tune. Actually I didn't know what tune it was until Wyatt acknowledged that he had taught Cosmo to whistle "Zip-A-Dee-Doo-Dah." As soon as I knew what Cosmo was trying to whistle, I whistled the whole song to her. Before long, she was whistling it with heart and soul, though not with all the right notes. She especially loved to whistle the part of tune that accompanies the second line of the verse:

> Zip-a-dee-doo-dah, zip-a-dee-ay,
> My, oh my, what a wonderful day.
> Plenty of sunshine heading my way,
> Zip-a-dee-doo-dah, zip-a-dee-ay.

Soon thereafter Cosmo learned the word whistle, which at first she pronounced, "whih-hul." She still doesn't pronounce it very clearly. But she certainly finds good use for the word.

COSMO: Cosmo wanna whistle?

73

BJC: Okay.
COSMO: Cosmo and Betty Jean wanna whistle?
BJC: Okay.

Then she whistles the opening "Zip-a-dee-doo-dah," I whistle "zip-a-dee-ay," and she whistles "My, oh my, what a wonderful day." She loves to do duets with me.

I taught Cosmo to whistle two other tunes: "Bridge on the River Kwai" and "Heigh-ho, heigh-ho," both of which she whistles well enough for them to be recognized by company. Sometimes she does an original and unrepeatable medley of the two. Often she will start out whistling one of the tunes and then compose something never before heard on earth. After whistling merrily all over the scale for a minute, she'll exclaim, "Wow! That's good whistle!" or "Wow! Whatta bird."

Whoever lives with Cosmo after I'm gone will think that Cosmo must be really, really old to be whistling the soundtracks to Walt Disney's 1937 animated film *Snow White and the Seven Dwarfs*, his 1946 *Song of the South*, and the 1957 *Bridge on the River Kwai*.

Cosmo whistles most in the mornings, maybe because she wakes up happy to start the new day. So after I get into the shower and have water pouring down my face, making whistling extremely difficult, she'll enter my bathroom and ask, "Betty Jean wanna whistle?" I'll reply, "Betty Jean wanna talk, okay?"

As I write, sitting at my desk in my study where I can gaze out at the woods and see the squirrels chase each other, Cosmo is perched on her cage behind me looking at the squirrels and monitoring my computer screen.

When I am home Cosmo and I can be together—conversing, whistling, playing, laughing, telling our jokes, or just enjoying the other's company—wherever I happen to be, because she has four full-sized cages in the house. Each cage is outfitted with rope toys, bell toys, and dishes for food and water, and each—except for the one in my study—has a playscape and a rope perch on top.

Number One Cage, which is white, is her roost cage. It is located in the sunroom, "Cosmo's room," where she has floor-to-ceiling windows and sliding glass doors to give her a view of life outdoors, as well as skylights to give her sunshine indoors. There, peering through the bars of her cage, Cosmo watches squirrels, chipmunks, and birds feed peaceably on the deck railing—peaceably, that is, until the dogs pop out of the doggy door to pursue them, causing them to dart under the deck, scamper into the woods, leap onto the trees, or fly away. Such is Cosmo's daytime entertainment when I'm gone.

I have arrived home at night to hear Cosmo say "squirrel" when none is in sight. Erin, the graduate student who videotaped Cosmo in my absence, wondered whether Cosmo might be reporting to me that she had seen a squirrel during the day. I decided to respond to her, "Cosmo saw a squirrel?" Lately, Cosmo has been telling me, at the end of the day, "Cosmo s...squirrel."

Number Two Cage, navy blue, is in the dining room by the kitchen, where Cosmo goes at meal time and at party time. From atop that cage she watches me cook, asking whenever I pull out something with which she's not familiar, "What's that?" I try to think of a generic label for it, such as "That's plate," "That's placemat," "That's silverware," "That's dinner for Betty Jean," "That's a bottle of Mat Garretson's 2004 Aisling Paso Robles Syrah." While I'm engaged in slicing and dicing, boiling and broiling, baking and basting, Cosmo carries on a lively conversation with me and keeps my attention focused on her. She talks, whistles, chirps, barks like the dogs, beeps like the microwave, and generally exhibits her pleasure with the situation. When I set the table in the dining room, she announces happily, "We're gonna have company!" She anticipates what will take place, and so she uses this improvisation of future tense to tell me about it. She dearly loves company. When the company arrives, she exclaims, "Company!" or "We've got company!"

If I'm not paying attention to her, if, for example, I have to take something out of the oven or off the stovetop, she climbs from her cage to the dining room table and flings forks and spoons off the table, cooing "*Ooooh*" or muttering "Cosmooooo." Or she walks quietly to a wine rack and chews the foil off a bottle of fine wine. Or she marches across the kitchen floor opening cabinet doors and disappearing into cabinets—except for her red tail feathers which give her location away—to poke around noisily among the pots and pans. She never poops inside the cabinets. She often heads into the cabinet under the sink because she likes to play with the old toothbrushes I store there. She knows where I keep everything—that is, everything within her reach. The pots and pans, the sponges and toothbrushes, the cans of dog food, the liquor, the garbage. She has fun scaring the dogs away from their own food dish. She hurries across the floor with her feathers ruffled and her wings akimbo to chase them out of the kitchen.

Number Three Cage, another white one, which I put together myself, is in my bedroom, where Cosmo goes to hang out with the dogs. In the evening she perches on the open door and teases me. She asks, "Betty Jean wanna cuddle?" I reluctantly get out of my comfortable leather chair to fetch her, and she hastens back into the cage shutting the cage door behind her. As soon as I settle back into my chair and return to my book, she emerges and says, "Cosmo wanna cuddle. Okay?" And she begs, "Come here, please. Cosmo wanna cuddle." I get up, and she goes back in the cage. We repeat this a few times. I convince myself that I'm getting good exercise. We go through the same routine when she asks to go to bed: "Cosmo wanna go to bed. Okay?" And she waits till I am two feet from her before she scuttles back into her cage and slams the door behind her. She must think that this is funny.

Now I say, "Cosmo wanna go to Betty Jean's chair?" She generally accepts that invitation, and she alternates preening by herself on the back of my chair and cuddling with me on the arm of my chair or in my lap. When we cuddle she closes her eyes in pleasure, or sleepiness, as I stroke her head and back. Other times she turns around and gives me a bite. The bite is not painful, but it's not pleasurable either. It's a signal for me not to do something. When she gets bitey, I know she's tired and I put her to bed.

One summer evening when she was about a year and a half, I put Cosmo to bed before dark. After all, in June darkness doesn't fall in Georgia until 9:00 or so, and parrots need at least ten hours of uninterrupted sleep. After I closed the door to her room and got settled in my bedroom for a movie, I heard, "Cosmo wanna water." I got up and changed the water in her water dish. I told her, "Good night," and closed the door to her room. When I had returned to my chair, I heard her speak again: "Cosmo wanna peanut." I entered her room and gave her a peanut. Next thing: "Cosmo wanna go up, okay?" She continues to play this game to this day. Now

I usually let her out again.

Number Four Cage, light blue, which I also put together and which is therefore missing its playscape—because I couldn't figure out how to attach it–can be moved around on the hardwood floor of my study. I usually place it behind my computer desk and too far from the bookshelf for Cosmo to reach the books, a few of which have bite marks. Cosmo perches on top of the cage and talks with me while I write. I have learned that I can keep up a running conversation with Cosmo while doing almost anything: writing, sending email, dressing, undressing, showering, eating, cooking, setting the table, reading, watching a movie, watching television, cleaning cages, wiping poop up off the floor—which elicits Cosmo's comment, "That's poop!"—and cleaning house.

I can also do lots of work with Cosmo perched on my left hand when she refuses to get off. I can put clothes into the washing machine, take dishes out of the dishwasher, set the table, speak on the phone, and do very slow email right-handedly.

One Sunday, Cosmo was chattering away with me during the half hour I was doing my online banking. Perched on top of Cage Number Four, Cosmo kept talking as I logged out of the bank website and pulled up on the screen a picture of a champion American Eskimo Dog. Then I heard Cosmo say suddenly, "That's doggy!" So all the time that I was doing my banking, Cosmo must have kept an eye on my computer screen. Finally she saw something interesting: a doggy. I was stunned. I immediately pulled a picture of a parrot up on the screen, but by that time she was climbing down off the cage to head toward the dogs' big water dish in the laundry room.

Another evening, after an hour of writing, I pulled

onto the computer screen a picture of an African Grey. Cosmo said from behind my back, "That's birdy!" And then, "That's Cosmo!" The picture was actually of an unknown African Grey, but Congo African Greys look very much alike to me, and evidently to Cosmo too. Cosmo thought she was seeing herself on the computer screen.

The next episode of Cosmo-and-the-computer is almost incredible, even to me, Cosmo's constant companion. I was at the computer looking at proofs of some photos of Cosmo and me taken by a University of Georgia photographer. Cosmo was perched on her cage behind me. I pulled up onto the screen a picture that showed Cosmo going for my ear—actually, going for my glasses, which she likes to take off my face. Cosmo, who had already said, "That's birdy," while we were looking at the proofs, said, "That hurt? Let go!" I had said, "Let go," in the studio, and she'd asked then, "That hurt?" Ten hours later, looking at the computer screen, Cosmo recognized herself in the action of going for my ear!

Believe it or not, Cosmo also has a Number Five Cage and a Number Six Cage. Number Five Cage is a small cage, about 14" x 16" x 22." It fits into the passenger's front seat in my Camry. One wintry Friday evening when Cosmo was about three years old, I was preparing to be picked up for dinner. Cosmo asked, "Where wanna gonna go?" I answered, "Betty Jean gonna go in a car." I said "in a car" because I wasn't going in my car. The phrase "in a car" stuck in Cosmo's mind. When I got home, Cosmo called out from the dark in her room, "Cosmo wanna go up," as she is wont to do when she hears me come home after she's gone to bed. When I brought her into my room, she said, "Cosmo wanna go in a car!" The only times she'd been in a car she had ridden in a doggy kennel to go to her vet. I decided to buy her one of those car cages recommended by *Bird Talk* magazine. Saturday was a snow day, but Sunday I went to the pet store and purchased Number Five Cage. We took a drive. She had a wonderful time.

Now she often says, "Cosmo wanna go in a car, okay?" And if the weather's warm—that is, between 68 and 78 degrees Fahrenheit—I'll consent to take her on errands. I never leave her in the car unless the weather is good and I can open the sunroof. As I carry her in Number Five Cage down the hall, she'll say to the dogs either "Doggies, wanna go in a car?" and I'll have to leash them up and take them with us, or "Doggies, stay home!"

One summer morning my friend Rodger saw Kaylee, Mary, and Cosmo with me at the filling station and asked where we were going. I answered that we were going to the Grand Canyon on a family vacation. Normally when Cosmo is riding in the car with me we're going out to dinner at the home of some of my dear friends who invite Cosmo too, as if she were my significant other. I guess she is, or rather, I'm hers. On the way, Cosmo will exclaim: "We're gonna have company!" By that she means that we will be with other people, and though she's a one-person bird, she definitely likes being with other people. After all, she is a flock animal.

You may wonder why I obey Cosmo, a bird. As much as I can—and within reason—I comply with her spoken wishes, because I want her to know that language works. I want her to know that the use of language enables her to manipulate her environment: to obtain peanuts, go to the kitchen, make people laugh, get a misting, get a kiss on her feathers, and get my rapt attention. When she speaks she has power, for she can tell me what to do, even though she's little and I'm big.

Number Six Cage has been parked for some time at the home of Margaret and Wyatt. It is about 22" x "22" x 36." Margaret and Wyatt have kept Cosmo on many occasions when I've gone out of town briefly, and she loves being at their house. Margaret cooks Cosmo's favorite vegetable especially for her: corn on the cob. Cosmo will get bits of corn all over her beak, and then, because she likes being neat and clean, will wipe off her beak vigorously on the rope perch. She'll do the same after I kiss her.

Imagine the difference for an African Grey Parrot between life in the wild and life in a human's home. In the rainforest, Congo African Greys live in large flocks; nest high up in tree holes, usually over water or on river islands; forage for food, gathering berries, nuts, seeds, and fruit from a variety of trees, including the palm oil tree; climb adeptly through tree canopies; and fly whenever and wherever they want. They watch out for predators; find a mate, reproduce, rear their young; interact rambunctiously with other flock members; and vocalize raucously at dawn and at dusk.

In the human home, the parrot spends many hours of the day confined to a cage with flight feathers clipped, receives dinner pre-selected in a bowl, lives for decades without predators but also without an avian mate, and often interacts only with other members of the household—human and non-human.

Because they are highly intelligent, African Greys kept as pets need to have daily excitement to compensate for the deprivation of the dangers and thrills of life in the wild. They must spend time outside the cage to get exercise and to have some control over their life, at least for a few hours every day. They must also have lots of social interaction to continue learning new things. Like smart people, they are life-long learners, and, like smart people, they suffer depression when they are isolated, permanently confined, or denied intellectual stimulation. They need to have entertainment, and they need to play. When they are unhappy, they pluck their feathers, even to the point of baldness.

I want Cosmo to be happy, and she seems to be. She greets the day joyously with whistles, chirps, and a vocalization of what I presume is going through her mind. If I awaken her before it gets light, I'll greet her with "Good morning" as I open her cage door, and she'll say sleepily, in the most loving voice conceivable, "Hellooooo."

I believe that there is not an absolute difference between humans and other species with regard to thinking and feeling, but rather a relative difference in cognitive ability and a difference in the content of thought and the expression of feeling. I'm not unaware of the enormous gap between brain surgery and telephone jokes, and between the discussion of stem cells and the discussion of peanuts, but I do marvel at the intelligence Cosmo demonstrates when discovering how to do things.

Maybe I'm a romantic. I like to contemplate the notion that all our planet's creatures have some sort of consciousness. They awaken in the morning—all except for the nocturnal ones and the hibernating ones—with something on their mind. Perhaps for a cardinal it's find food, or mate, or build a nest, or lay an egg, or sit on the nest, or get food for the chicks. Perhaps for a fox it's go hunting, kill a rabbit. For a rattle snake it may be lie in the sun. For a squirrel it may be go to the lady's deck to see what she's left me on the railing.

And don't all the planet's creatures have some fun?

Hawks must enjoy soaring high in the sky on a sunny day. Whales must enjoy cavorting in the water.

My favorite sentence from Darwin's *Origin of Species* appears in the book's final paragraph:

> It is interesting to contemplate a tangled bank, clothed with many plants of many kinds, with birds singing on the bushes, with various insects flitting about, and with worms crawling through the damp earth, and to reflect that these elaborately constructed forms, so different from each other, and dependent upon each other in so complex a manner, have all been produced by laws acting around us.

All "dependent upon each other"—and all the animals, I would add, aware of other animals in their local tangled bank. They view some as predators, some as prey, and some as fellow residents of their land.

What do you suppose these animals think of us humans? I know that a particular squirrel watches me through the windows of my house in the morning waiting patiently for me to bring out the squirrel seed, which she shares with the birds. She knows what I look like and what time of day I go to the kitchen. She also knows my dogs. I wonder whether we are in her dreams. The deer, the raccoons, and the foxes that live behind my house in the woods must have some opinions of my neighbors and me, who have constructed houses in their territory. In their dreams, are we dangerous monsters? Or simply fellow residents of their land?

Each of these creatures has memories, just as each of us humans has memories. Our memories of family and friends, and what we have done in our life and what has been done to us, where we have been, whom we have known, whom we have loved, and whom we have feared—all these memories go into what constitutes our "self." It is the same with our non-human fellow residents of the land. We humans feel bad when we hurt each other's feelings, in part because we know our action enters the other's memories of us. Should we not feel similar guilt and sorrow when we threaten, harm, or frighten the earth's animals? Would we feel bad if we realized that our actions had entered their memories, too? As surely as they remember where they can find food and shelter, they remember what has been done to them, what has been given to them, and what has been taken away. Like us, they remember the people they have encountered, good and bad. Mockingbirds, for example, try to chase away those individual humans who once banded them.

Just think of the trillions of creatures in our global tangled bank, besides the six and a half billion humans, having the same needs and pleasures, looking for mates, foraging or hunting with their kind, all interacting with others in a struggle to survive and reproduce, and having memories and dreams of each other and of us humans. The vision gives me goose bumps.

These creatures also play, at least when they are juvenile. They have fun with each other, as anybody living in a household with parrots, dogs, cats, ferrets, guinea pigs, hamsters, or rabbits can tell you. My dogs Mary and Kaylee play with each other. They play mock-fighting games, pouncing on each other and grabbing each other by the neck. They chase each other, groom each other, and scare each other. They each assume the widely recognized posture for playing, with their head on the ground and their butt in the air, a posture they recognize as an invitation to fun, even when it is assumed by a human.

And Mary and Cosmo play with each other. They play chase, keep away, and scare-you. Chase usually involves Cosmo chasing Mary, not vice versa, with Mary allowing Cosmo to get quite near her. Scare-you involves Cosmo and Mary getting closer and closer to each other until beak and nose just about touch and Cosmo opens her beak to scare Mary. Keep away involves Mary bringing a toy to Cosmo, grabbing it, and then putting it back beside Cosmo for Cosmo to grab it. They take turns. In each of these games, Mary, who weighs eleven pounds more than Cosmo, lets Cosmo win. They appear to be having fun, and they like each other. They are friends.

One day I saw Mary dangle a formerly stuffed animal—a cloth monkey that had long since lost its button eyes and its stuffing—over the edge of the bed so that Cosmo, reaching up as high as she could from the floor, could grab it. Cosmo failed to grab it, and Mary dropped it. Then they both lost interest in the monkey, for the game was over. Another day, after observing Mary get leashed, Cosmo took Mary for a walk down the hall. Cosmo picked up the end of Mary's leash in her beak, and Mary, aware of this, proceeded very, very slowly down the hall, dragging the leash on the floor, so that Cosmo could keep up with her. Cosmo did, scurrying after Mary with the leash in her beak for four or five feet before she dropped it. That seemed to be fun for both.

Play is necessary for the intellectual development of almost all animals, at least until they reach sexual maturity. For everybody, including humans, play is an enjoyable means of learning how to be an adult without the responsibilities and dangers. Just imagine: Juvenile squirrels playing with each other are learning how to be mature, well-behaved adult squirrels, responsible for

Cosmo takes Mary for a walk.

raising their own families one day. Play is also, according to animal behaviorist Alex Hawes, an activity that strengthens social bonds among members of a group, replacing aggression with cooperation. In my household, play has turned us four individuals into a flock, a pack, and a family.

Cosmo seems to be playing when she mimics the smoke alarm, the telephone, the answering machine, the dogs' bark, and the truck backing up. But I can't tell whether her amusement—if that's what it is—comes from my responses to her mimicry or from the act of mimicry itself. Pretending that she was not making the peeps of the smoke alarm or the *rrrring* of the phone when I'd try to catch her doing it shows her desire to fool me. She must take fun in that. Yet she also mimics the sounds of her environment when I'm not around—in the morning before I come into her room; during the day, according to Erin's video camera; and whenever she notices an unfamiliar noise that interests her, such as a siren.

African Greys have a natural ability to mimic, and they can mimic unfamiliar noises their whole lives. In the wild, Greys reportedly imitate birds of other species, unlike some other parrots who tend to imitate only birds of their own. So what is the evolutionary advantage to accurate vocal mimicry for African Greys? Harvard researcher Michael Schindlinger writes, "Imitative vocal learning is also a reliable social display of neural functions—requiring good hearing, memory, and muscle control for sound production—that may be under consideration by a potential mate or ally." Is that showing off? Maybe Cosmo is showing off to me—and to my friends. Maybe she is proving to herself that she is "whatta bird." Whatever her aim, she loves doing it and she is expert at it.

African Greys don't reach sexual maturity until age six, more or less, so in the wild they have a long time to play and to educate themselves on how to be a parrot, which they do by imitating the behavior—and, I assume, copying the bird calls—of their elders in the flock. Unlike hummingbirds and honey bees, Greys do not hatch with survival skills ready for use; they must acquire them in their first few years of life. I think that is why Greys and other parrots bred in captivity adapt well to our human homes. By interacting with us humans when they're young, observing our behavior, and imitating our communication with one another, they educate themselves on how to be a pet parrot. I leave the question of the relationship between high intelligence and lengthy sexual immaturity to the experts, but I do believe that parrots' extended period of play and learning correlates with their ability to live happily with a human family and, in some species, with their ability to talk.

Wild-caught parrots, who have learned how to be a parrot in the wild, will rarely adapt happily to the human home. For wild-caught parrots, the human home represents captivity and dispossession.

Cosmo has expanded my awareness of the rich natural life around us, and she has done this by talking with me. She has instilled in me much greater empathy than I used to have for all the birds, squirrels, deer, and turtles with whom we share precious space on earth. I have always tried to see the world from the viewpoint of my dogs, who love me, want me to come home early to feed them, and want me to go to bed at a reasonable hour so that they can sleep. Now when I watch armadillos dig for insects in the ground, or woodpeckers peck holes in my cedar siding, or deer bound over the uneven terrain of my woods, I know they too have intentions and expectations, and I try to think their thoughts with them. I'm not as successful at this as I would like to be.

I am more successful with Cosmo, who lets me know what her intentions and expectations are. When I write that she is laughing or telling jokes or having fun, I am aware that I am attributing human emotions, thoughts, and humor to her. I just can't see an absolute difference between her little self and mine.

4. *I Love You!*

COSMO: "*Cosmo wanna dance, okay?*"
BJC: "*Okay, step up.*"
[I dance with Cosmo on my hand. Cosmo sways with the music.]
COSMO: "*I love you!*"

*C*osmo is an ambassador of the non-human community to the human community, and she brings great tidings.

I take Cosmo—in her travel cage in the right front seat of my car—to visit schools, such as Oconee County Elementary, and other places to educate people about the African Greys' remarkable vocal, communicative, and intellectual abilities. I do it not just for fun, although I do take pleasure in introducing Cosmo to people, but in a modest mission to make a better world. I hope that greater comprehension of the mental abilities of non-human animals like Cosmo will lead to greater capacity for empathy with all the other residents of our planet: avian, canine, feline, bovine, amphibian, human, reptilian, etcetera.

I teach and write about holism, having been influenced by the late Gene Odum, my close friend at the University of Georgia who developed the ecosystem concept. Gene argued that the human community and the rest of nature compose an interactive, interdependent whole and that we need to understand the importance of cooperation, or symbiosis, in all relationships. Gene got me obsessed with thinking about how our Western society is gradually developing a more holistic outlook, which I consider healthier for the whole of nature than the way we used to think about humans and animals. For many centuries, we humans have assumed that our species was created to have dominion over the planet's other species. We dichotomized the world—into spirit and matter; soul and body; self and world; humans and nature; intellect and instinct, us and them—and ranked the creatures in it. From Greek Antiquity until at least the late nineteenth century we conceived of an absolute difference between humans, with souls, and animals, without. And we viewed the animal kingdom as a hierarchy, with us on top just below God, and chimpanzees, dogs, dolphins, squirrels, armadillos, birds, fish, frogs, bees, plants, and algae beneath us, in more or less descending order. We even ranked the races and the sexes: whites over yellows, browns, reds, and blacks; men over women. Lots of folks still think this way, even though Darwin's theory of evolution by natural selection discredited it a hundred and fifty years ago.

But the times are a changin'—as we first heard from Bob Dylan in 1964. In the late twentieth century civil rights leaders awakened the country to the detrimental social consequences of those habits of thought, which led most obviously to racism and patriarchy. They showed that the hierarchical model justified our dominance and control over everybody we ranked lower than ourselves; and that the dualism, an inclination to consider ourselves in opposition to others, kept us from developing empathy with anybody unlike "us," whoever "us" might be at the time. On the same grounds, animal liberationists condemned our "speciesism," a word coined by Richard Ryder in 1973 for our willingness to cause suffering for individuals of other species that we would prohibit for individuals of our own. Environmentalists pointed out that by treating nature as exterior and in-

Cosmo and her friends pose for a Christmas photo.

ferior to humans we saw no harm to ourselves in polluting the soil, the plants, the air, and the water. We did not notice the effect of our pollution on whatever walked over it, ran across it, climbed up it, flew through it, or swam in it.

Now we notice that harming other constituents of our planetary ecosystem brings harm to ourselves.

I try to get students to see every species, even every organism, and every river, lake, and mountain as an interconnected part of our planetary ecosystem. In this model we see that we all need each other and that the loss or suffering of any of us affects in some way or other the wellbeing of the rest of us, so we had better cooperate. We see the value of even the algae to the rest of us. We will therefore want to protect our natural environment and preserve its biodiversity. The holistic model replaces the dualist "us-versus-them" attitude with "us all"—the understanding that we're all in this world together. I hope that when we recognize our interdependence we will not only respect the many different peoples of the global political community and endeavor to ensure their health but also endeavor to ensure the health of the other members of our planet's biotic community. In my ecocriticism class I teach the essay "The Land Ethic," which the Wisconsin forester Aldo Leopold wrote some seventy years ago, and which is a foundational document of American environmentalism. The students really take to Leopold's message that we need to extend our ethical community to include the land and then develop a "land ethic" to change the role of Homo sapiens "from conqueror of the land-community to plain member and citizen of it." As of now, we're still conquerors, and we still think of ourselves as "us" and of the other components of the web of life as the inferior "them."

But as we come to appreciate the lively minds of our non-human fellow residents of the earth, we will include them in our ethical community. I hope.

This is where Cosmo comes in, a little emissary from aviankind to humankind. I take Cosmo to my class at least once during the semester to arouse the students' possibly dormant ability to empathize with animals and see the world from their viewpoint. And I take her to other classes whenever I—or we—get invited.

When Cosmo chirped "Telephone for bird!" to the Oconee County Elementary School children, the eight-year-old future leaders of our society laughed as hard as they would have laughed had one of their own class told the joke. For that short time, Cosmo was a plain member and citizen of their class. And they were plain members and citizens of Cosmo's flock.

What the children learned that day they will probably not forget, and they will probably become more concerned about animal welfare than they would otherwise have been.

Cosmo can teach children what she thinks about: for example, squirrels, doggies, company, kitchen, and me; what she wants, such as peanuts, a shower, and a ride in the car; and what she considers fun, like playing telephone, talking to company, going to work, and splashing in the dogs' big water dish.

> COSMO: "Wanna talk?"
> CHILDREN: "Okay."
> COSMO: "Let's talk. How are you?"
> CHILDREN: "Fine, thank you. How are you?'
> COSMO: "Cosmo is a good good bird! Wanna whistle? *Whee whew*!"

Cosmo can show children what she, "a good good bird," has in mind. Children certainly understand Cosmo's values, for Cosmo's values are a bit like theirs.

What a great future we will have if a whole generation of children learn that birds and chimpanzees, dogs, dolphins, squirrels, and armadillos, even fish and frogs—though maybe not plants—all have something on their mind and all feel pleasure and pain. Children capable of empathizing with animals unlike themselves will be capable of empathizing with people unlike themselves. They may become better diplomats, politicians, friends, neighbors, and family members, as well as better citizens of the world and protectors of the planet, than have been people of my generation. They may develop a land ethic and understand that abuse of parts of the land ultimately damages the whole.

Sometimes I think that all of the world's problems—well, maybe not all, but many—could be solved if humans just had a greater capacity for empathy.

Cosmo can also teach us that animals worry. In the

spring of 2008, one Saturday afternoon while we were on our walk, my little dog Mary was bitten by a big black dog running loose in the neighborhood. Mary spent Sunday in pain, evidently in need of veterinary care, so at 7:30 Monday morning I took Mary in the car with me to visit Ralph, our vet. Ralph fixed Mary up, as he always does, and recommended that Mary be hospitalized in his clinic, since for the next four days Mary would have to wear an Elizabethan collar. Ralph was well acquainted with my family, and he knew that Cosmo would have been irresistibly tempted to take a bite out of the collar.

On Tuesday evening after work, I walked into the house to this:

COSMO: "Mary?'
BJC: "Hello, Cosmo!"
COSMO: "Mary go in a car?"
BJC: "Yes, Mary go in a car. Mary be back soon."

Cosmo was using the only language she knew to find out where Mary had gone. I brought Mary home on Thursday evening. After getting released from her cage, Cosmo followed Mary into my bedroom and greeted her: "Hi!" Cosmo had thought about Mary during the week and had missed her.

Cosmo expresses affection in various ways. I often play music for Cosmo—and me—on Cosmo's CD player. The first CD I played for Cosmo, over and over because the lead melody haunted my imagination, was *Cristofori's Dream* by David Lanz. I would put Cosmo on my left hand, where I usually hold her, and sweep giant arcs in space to the rhythm of that gorgeous waltz, "Cristofori's Dream." While swaying to the music, I'd say, "Cosmo wanna dance?" and Cosmo would invariably emit a long whistle of delight. Then, after a minute or so,

Cosmo would say either "I love you" or "Wanna cuddle?" And she did wanna cuddle. I usually end our dancing with a gentle massage. I sit down, and she flops herself over on my lap, relaxes completely, and closes her eyes in anticipation.

Cosmo appears to love me in the same way that Mary and Kaylee do. All three show affection by kissing, and all three like having their heads rubbed. Just as we humans do. Do all animals—or at least all furry and feathery animals—like kissing and cuddling?

I googled "animals kissing" on the internet and found pictures of dogs, cats, pandas, seals, tigers, hamsters, rhinos, horses, and birds of all kinds kissing each other. Also dogs kissing cats, dolphins kissing dogs, and humans kissing just about everything that lives and breathes, except armadillos, fish, frogs, and bees.

The third-graders at Oconee County Elementary School loved seeing Cosmo and me kiss.

I had had Cosmo for only three months when I took her back to the pet store to get her flight feathers clipped for the first time. She spotted on a perch the other young African Grey with whom she'd spent her chickhood, and who had not yet found a home. Cosmo leaned forward, almost falling off my hand, to go to the bird. I let her onto the perch, and the two of them met each other with cheeps of excitement. Then they kissed. They each put their little black tongue into the other's beak. I felt thrilled and privileged to witness this intimate act of affection, but a little sad to realize that the parrots had cared for each other when I had taken away one of them. They had probably been nest mates in Florida before they traveled together to Athens.

At the age of three, Cosmo received an invitation for a play date with a seven-month-old African Grey named

Ruby. I took Cosmo over in her travel cage and then let her perch on top of it, since Ruby was perched atop hers. When Cosmo spotted Ruby, she said, "That's a birdy!" and then climbed onto her cage. They kissed—a good, extended, tongue-in-beak kiss. What a first date! But by the second date, a year later, Cosmo had lost interest in Ruby. So it goes.

Once when I left her with Margaret and Wyatt in her cage at their house, Cosmo said to me plaintively, as I told her good-bye, "Cosmo wanna go in a car!" She knew that I was leaving her, and she wanted to go home with me. On other occasions when I've said good-bye to her there, she has simply looked at me and said cheerily, "Good-bye." She likes Margaret and Wyatt very much, for she has a fine time at their house talking, whistling, *rrrring*ing the phone, and eating cashews, but when I pick her up after a few days out of town, she is sweet beyond belief. On one occasion, she immediately asked, "Wanna cuddle?"

I miss Cosmo, Mary, and Kaylee when I'm out of town, and they miss me, I know. As every dog-owner can tell you, a dog will shower you with sloppy kisses when you return to her after having been gone for a length of time. Mary and Kaylee will jump up and down and run circles around me. Cosmo will invite me to kiss her feathers:

COSMO: "Betty Jean wanna kiss feathers?"
BJC: "Yes, Cosmo. I wanna kiss feathers. *Smooch.* Thank you."

Now why would a rational, or mostly rational, adult human want to kiss her bird's feathers? That's not hard for me to answer, even forgetting about how nice they

96

smell. I love Cosmo. That is, I want to touch her, comfort her, protect her, entertain her, hold her near me, let her know I care for her, and keep her caring for me. At dawn her joyful responses to the awakening birds in the woods stir me to consciousness, and soon I hear her calling me: "Cosmo wanna go up!" My heart flutters as I remember that that little parrot is awaiting eagerly my entrance into her room. When I let Cosmo out of her cage, I kiss her beak and then her feathers. She kisses me back.

I am convinced that she is feeling pleasure when she does it.

So how arrogant must we humans be to assert that we are distinct from non-humans in the possession of "consciousness"? I believe that almost everybody on this planet who walks, runs, climbs, flies, or swims has some sort of mental life, though we humans are the only species capable of writing poetry, composing symphonies, discussing the origin of species, determining the composition of stars, and inventing weapons of mass destruction.

I wonder whether our society's intellectual struggle to define our uniqueness in the animal kingdom is a result of the shock that Darwin's theory of evolution by natural selection gave to Western civilization in 1859. Before the publication of the *Origin of Species*, most people did not question the religious notion of the human soul, "a person's spiritual as opposed to corporeal nature," according to the *Oxford English Dictionary*. We believed that humans had souls, and that dogs and birds and chimps and dolphins did not, that the soul was separate from the body, that it was connected to God, and that it had everlasting life. We humans were confident that we were unique, because we knew that God had created us in his own image. We could be righteous conquerors of the land-community because the Bible prescribed our dominion over the fish of the sea, the fowl of the air, the cattle, and every creeping thing that crept upon the earth. But in 1859, Darwin's claim that we humans had evolved like all other organisms according to natural laws made thoughtful readers ask whether we humans really had souls. In a nature characterized by continuous change, what was a soul anyway?

Now we talk about "consciousness," which seems to me a post-Darwinian replacement for "soul." Philosophers discuss whether animals have consciousness, or more specifically, self-consciousness.

In the last few decades researchers in the field of animal cognition have dramatically expanded our knowledge of the mental abilities of non-human animals, overturning longstanding definitions for what is uniquely human. We can no longer say that what marks us as human is tool use, as we once did, because researchers have observed monkeys and crows fashioning tools to get food. Nor can we say it's speech, since researchers have heard whales communicating with members of their own pod in songs that employ grammar. Nor can we say it's self-awareness, since researchers have shown that elephants recognize themselves in a mirror. I was not surprised to find out about the elephants' self-awareness, for Cosmo recognizes herself in the mirror.

We have learned that animals are capable of deceiving us intentionally, which, as Virginia Morell writes *in National Geographic's* March 2008 issue on animal minds, requires the ability "to attribute intentions to the other person and predict that person's behavior." So those animals must spend some time figuring out us humans. Cosmo must spend a lot of time thinking about me, for she is quite deceptive when she wants to be. For instance, she says, "Cosmo wanna shower," and walks down the hall to the laundry room. Out of my sight, she quietly makes sawdust of the baseboard. As soon as she hears me approach the laundry room calling "Cosmo, where are you?" she scurries to the dogs' water dish and announces "Shower for Cosmo!" I leave, and I hear her scurry back to the baseboard she's been working on. Cosmo knows that she is doing something she's not supposed to do, and she doesn't want me to see her doing it.

And she is capable of manipulating me to fulfill her wishes. One early morning at breakfast time, while perched on top of the cage in my bedroom, Cosmo said, "Cosmo wanna go to kitchen!" Then she gave me a pretend-bite when I reached up to take her on my hand. I immediately said, "Bad bird!" and walked away down the hall. She called out, "I love you!" I returned to give her a ride to the kitchen.

We commonly understand "consciousness" as what humans have that animals don't. The *Oxford English Dictionary* gives as the first definition of *consciousness*: "Internal knowledge or conviction, esp. of one's own guilt, innocence, deficiencies, etc." According to that definition, Cosmo doesn't have consciousness, because she shows no awareness of her own deficiencies. None whatsoever. But she does mutter after giving me a hard bite, "Cosmo bad bird. Go back in cage," which is what I've said to her on occasion, though in an elevated tone of voice. Cosmo has an idea of what is good behavior and bad behavior, at least in her house.

What's the point of proving that Cosmo—or any other animal, for that matter–doesn't have consciousness? It's as pointless to me as proving that Cosmo doesn't have a soul. It's finally a matter of semantics.

I prefer to talk of *selves*. It's more democratic, since everyone's got one. And without the divine distinction between those beings with souls and those without, or the secular distinction between those with consciousness and those without, we all become—theoretically—plain members and citizens of the land-community.

I have heard Irene Pepperberg's research on African Grey communication and cognition criticized for being based on a sample of one. Actually, that criticism is not fair, in my opinion, because it fails to take into account the effect emotional attachments have on individuals' learning capabilities—whether the individuals are avian or human or canine or simian. Nobody could teach fifty African Greys the skills that Irene taught Alex, because the fifty parrots would not develop the intimate bond with Irene that Alex did. Fifty parrots would behave as a flock, not as fifty individual students. Can you picture fifty African Greys patiently sitting on fifty perches in a classroom taking turns answering the question, "How many red blocks?"

So one lesson we can take away from Irene's work is the influence relationships have on an individual's motivation. A more important lesson, however, is the influence language has on an individual's intellectual development.

Irene enabled Alex to have thoughts he would not have had in the rain forest, for she gave Alex language he would not have had in the rain forest. In teaching him, in English, to distinguish shapes and colors and numbers, she was actually teaching him to think like a human. She made Alex intellectually different from his African relatives and unique among parrots and other animals for the abilities he developed under her tutelage. Alex apparently enjoyed his education immensely, in part because he liked to please Irene, but also in part because he found intellectual activity enjoyable. Don't we all?

By giving language to our non-human companions we are not only socializing and civilizing them to please us, in our language, but also giving them our human conceptual framework to understand the multitudinous sights and sounds of their—our—environment.

Irene was not alone in teaching a non-human to think like a human. Francine Patterson gave Koko the lowland gorilla "Gorilla Sign Language" and enabled Koko to lie and to tell jokes. Ernst von Glasersfeld and his colleagues at Yerkes National Primate Centre gave Lana the chimpanzee a language of lexigrams, "Yerkish," and enabled Lana to sequence words grammatically to express her wishes. I salute Irene Pepperberg, Francine Patterson, Ernst von Glasersfeld, and other pioneers in the field of animal cognition for showing us the cognitive flexibility of these non-humans. I hope that their work leads to the expansion of our ethical community to include non-humans.

I gave Cosmo spoken English, or Cosmish, to enable her to tell me what a bird thinks, and I discovered that she thinks a lot like me, or maybe like me when I was two or three years old. Am I looking at a feathery version of myself? I wanted Cosmo to disclose her avian thoughts in my language, and instead she disclosed thoughts like my own. Did she already think like me or did I teach her to think like me? To laugh—or make the sound of laughter—at the same things I laugh at? To pay attention to the same occurrences that I pay attention to? To use my voice with my intonation and decibel level? To enjoy my friends? To share my value system of good and bad, knowing what being a good bird and being a bad bird mean? Sometimes she says "Cosmooooo," in mockery, I think, of the sigh of exasperation I make when I catch her being bad. Then she laughs.

I wonder what is going on in Cosmo's mind that she cannot communicate to me in English.

After living with Cosmo for a few years, I have come to believe that Benjamin Lee Whorf was right: that language conditions the thoughts and behaviors of its speakers. If we consider his theory, known as the Sapir-Whorf Hypothesis, in relation to language acquisition in animals, we can understand that by giving Cosmo the ability to communicate in English I am teaching her to think like a human, an English-speaking human. We humans should stand in awe of these little avian individuals who speak with us in our language using a syrinx.

Cosmo expresses what's on her mind in English whether or not she means to communicate with me. Once when she took a fall in her cage—Number Three Cage, in my bedroom—she exclaimed, "Ow!" She will routinely comment on where she is going, whether or not I'm nearby, as when she heads towards my bedroom declaring sotto voce, "Cosmo go to Betty Jean's room." She will call "Mary, come here!" when Mary is outside barking, and then will comment to herself, "That's doggy bark." Once she said, "That's paper for Cosmo's poop!" I don't know whether she was referring to the paper in her cage or the paper towels she presumes are dedicated to cleaning up her poop.

A camera set up by Erin to capture Cosmo's speech when I was not home caught Cosmo looking out to the deck and saying to herself, "Squirrel!" Even though Erin's camera didn't record the squirrel, I am guessing that Cosmo was commenting on a squirrel she had spied outside.

I brought Cosmo into my English-language-mediated world, and she adapted to it, with delight. What do we learn from these achievements by our non-human companions? We learn that they have a capacity for thinking and feeling way beyond what we previously attributed to them. I don't feel the need to claim that Cosmo is as smart as a young human or as competent in verbal expression. In fact, I don't see any reason at all to evaluate the intelligence of animals on a unilinear scale, especially a scale designed to measure human intelligence. Why should we teach parrots to think like humans and to speak our language, and then ignore their other avian abilities and declare triumphantly that we're smarter than they?

Erin gave her Master's thesis, which she wrote under the direction of psychologist and animal behaviorist Dorothy Fragaszy, the title "An African Grey Parrot's Vocal Production Varies across Social Context." In her research she sought answers to the following questions:

How does Cosmo use language? Are her requests contextually appropriate? When she is alone, does she vocalize more verbally or nonverbally? Does she make contact calls during times of separation from Betty Jean?

How is Cosmo regulating her social interaction with Betty Jean? Does she exhibit turn-taking in her verbal interaction with Betty Jean, or does she interrupt? Does she exhibit humor?

To gather data during the past year, Erin set up a video camera in Cosmo's room about eight feet from her cage and recorded four hours in each of these situations: 1) Cosmo and me together in Cosmo's room; 2) Cosmo in her room with me and another person—neither of us paying attention to her; 3) Cosmo in her room alone— while I am in another room; and 4) Cosmo alone—while I am outside the house.

Erin was looking for evidence of deliberate use of language, expressed through body-positioning, turn-taking in dialogue, and context-appropriate requests.

Gathering the data was not as easy as it might appear. The first time Erin videotaped conversations between Cosmo and me she couldn't tell our voices apart when she watched the videotape back in her lab. Erin had to discard those tapes and adjust the distance of the camera from the cage to see whether Cosmo's beak was moving when Erin heard utterances such as "Hello. How are you? Fine, thank you. How are you?" and "Cosmo is a good bird!" We also had a problem recording Cosmo when Erin and I were talking and, ostensibly, not paying attention to her. I didn't have the heart, at first, not to respond to Cosmo's interruptions of the conversation Erin and I were having. When Cosmo interrupted us with "How are you?" I'd look up and say, quickly, "Fine thank you, how are you?" Erin had to discard those tapes too. From then on, Erin and I alternated reading sentences from printed matter to simulate a conversation. She did not allow me to look at Cosmo.

Erin made the following report to her graduate committee:

Preliminary results include frequent non-word vocalizations when alone or ignored, phrase choice and placement that are arguably similar to human persistence and persuasion, re-occurring phrases referencing subject and owner location with frequent requests for interaction when owner not in the room, and possible behavioral indications of frustration at being ignored. These results suggest the subject deliberately uses language as a tool to regulate the owner's attention and physical proximity.

Erin noticed that in Situation 1) when Cosmo and I were in the room together, Cosmo talked a lot; took turns in the conversation, that is, Cosmo said something, waited for me to answer, I answered, and then Cosmo said something else; looked at me when we were communicating; made utterances that could be described as funny and then laughed; said "Please" to intensify a request, as in "Wanna go up, please"; said "Look!" to get my attention; was persistent in her demands, as in "Wanna go up, please," "Cosmo wanna go up," "Wanna go up!" "Cosmo wanna go up, please"; and ceased asking for whatever she wanted once she got it. As Erin put it,

> Many of Cosmo's denied requests were posed again with words like "look," "please," or "okay." Similarly, denied requests to be let out of her cage were often repeated after being primed with units such as "Cosmo don't bite okay" or "Wanna be a good bird."

In Situation 2), when I was conversing with company and ignoring her, Cosmo tried to get my attention with bell-ringing, repetition of phrases, and birdy chirps. While recording her in this situation, Erin and I observed that Cosmo would usually preen herself quietly after failing to get attention from us. But on one occasion Cosmo made a big ruckus with her bell to interrupt what she must have considered a long, tedious conversation. I would have done the same thing if I had had a bell.

In Situation 3), when she was stuck in her cage and I was in another room, Cosmo made "insistent contact calls with amplified volume," as Erin said. I say, Cosmo is hollering to me: "I'm here!" "Where are you?" "Here I am!" "Come here!" In her thesis, Erin wrote:

> My main thematic prediction was that Cosmo would be more likely to reference her own spatial location and that of B.J. during times of visual separation. The data supported this prediction, as evidenced by differences across condition in the relative utterance frequencies involving that theme. The contextual specificity with which Cosmo uses these units is a strong indication that she uses them deliberately. Moreover, she typically uttered the units with an amplified voice (similar to B.J.'s), and the vocalizations were persistent, repetitive, and frequently solicited vocal response from B.J. Discrete vocalizations used to solicit vocal interaction and maintain social contact is Bergman and Reinisch's (2006) functional definition of a contact call. Cosmo's vocal behavior supported the notion that she uses English words as an equivalent of contact calls.

Erin said that Cosmo appeared to be requesting interaction and interrupting whatever I might be doing.

In Situation 4), when she was alone in the house, Cosmo mimicked the phone ring, made bird calls, and tried out new words. Erin noticed that on the day Cosmo looked out to the deck and said "Squirrel" to herself, Cosmo said "Squirrel" to me when I came home twenty minutes later.

While I assume that Cosmo knows what's funny, Erin as a scientist does not make that assumption. Erin makes no assumptions, actually. She says that Cosmo may simply have learned from repeated experience how to apply phrases that elicit laughter to manipulate others' behavior and to buffer a negative situation. I say that Cosmo does use humor, which I think she got from me, to get out of trouble, as when I scold her for biting and she finds herself "back in cage." After pleading unsuccessfully, "Cosmo wanna go up, Cosmo be a good bird, Cosmo don't bite," Cosmo may say, "Mary has feathers!" to get me to laugh and let her out of her cage. Or if I am ignoring her, as I do rarely—extremely rarely—Cosmo may mimic the phone, "*Rrrring rrrring*," and then say "Telephone for Betty Jean!" to get my attention.

In her presentation to her graduate committee, Erin said that Cosmo "is not a tape-recorder" and that she uses language "for facultative and social reasons," to achieve her goal of social interaction and to keep up a close relationship with me. Erin concluded that maintaining social contact with me was very important to Cosmo. I conclude that Cosmo loves me.

The studies of animal cognition show that the animals with whom we are interacting have a lively mental life that often features us, their human companions, though of course not exclusively. If they are learning from us, they think of us. If they are trying to deceive us, they think of us. And if they are physically abused by us, when they are confined to a small cage in a zoo by us, for example, they think of us—and without affection. While we observe them, they observe us.

Cosmo has mastered the social skill of turn-taking in dialogue, so in our conversations she must be thinking of me and waiting for my response to whatever she has said. She thinks about me when I am gone, when she is separated from me in the house, when she wants to go in a car, when she wants water or food, when she wants to tell me something, and when she wants some fun. "*Rrrring!*" She makes that *rrrring* for me.

We must realize that all of us—humans and animals alike—are thinking all the time about one another, sometimes with pleasure, sometimes with fear, sometimes with affection. We all have an active mental life. The struggle to survive and find pleasure requires it.

5. Cosmo Is a Good, Good Bird

COSMO: Cosmo wanna go to bed.
BJC: Okay, just a minute.
COSMO: Time to go to bed!
BJC: Okay. Okay.
COSMO: Cosmo wanna cuddle. Cosmo be a good bird.
BJC: Okay. Step up.

At bedtime, Cosmo's bedtime, that is, about 8 o'clock in the winter, 9 o'clock in the summer, Cosmo wants a massage. For fifteen minutes or so—or until the muscles of my fingers give out—she perches on the arm of my chair while I stroke her head, rub her neck and back, and gently tug at her beautiful red tail feathers. She twists this way and that to get me to touch all the parts of her body she wants touched, and she closes her eyes contentedly. Finally, she is ready to go to bed. I put her in her cage in the darkened sunroom, give her a kiss, tell her "Good night. I love you," and softly shut the door.

I get as much out of this evening ritual as Cosmo does. The ritual calms her down, and it calms me down too.

While we cuddle, I try to imagine what Cosmo's feelings must be, as she subjects her sixteen-ounce body to the fingers of the adult human who controls her life. To fully relax, she must be confident that I will never hurt her. She must trust me completely. She may consider me her servant, a human who pets her, feeds her, plays with her, talks with her, whistles with her, and understands her wishes, when she expresses them in English. What does she think about as she enjoys my caresses? She is certainly thinking about something. Who on this planet is not?

I hope that I have given Cosmo pleasure. She has obviously given me pleasure.

We humans have been keeping parrots for our pleasure for millennia. Egyptians kept African Grey parrots 3500 years ago, as shown in hieroglyphics. Aristotle kept a parrot named *Psittace*, from which the scientific name for parrots, *Psittacine*, is derived, 2500 years ago. The Romans brought African Greys to Europe, but they also ate them. King Henry VIII owned an African Grey. So did Marie Antoinette. And these days so do many Europeans and Americans.

Yarns and tall tales about parrots abound. Not a week goes by that I do not receive from one friend or another a parrot joke or a web address for a You Tube parrot video, like that of the dancing cockatoo. Parrots fascinate us because they speak like us and look like birds, occupying a unique niche between humans and the rest of the animal kingdom. Their ability to talk inclines all of us Dr. Doolittle wannabes to see them as native informants capable of enlightening us with their special knowledge.

Tribal customs in Tanzania mandate that upon the death of a family's patriarch the eldest son inherits the parrot, considered the family's dearest possession. Since the eldest son is supposed to remain on the homestead, this practice ensures that the parrot stay with the house. In other words, the parrot may not be evicted. An African colleague told me that African Greys in particular were prized because they spoke in the voice of the departed—they kept the dead person's spirit alive for successive generations in the family.

I like to think that my relatives who will have

Cosmo enjoys receiving a massage.

Cosmo when I'm gone will recollect my laugh when they hear Cosmo's.

Cosmo may live another forty years or more. The lifespan of parrots is related to their size. For example, Macaws kept as pets tend to live from fifty to a hundred years, cockatoos from forty to eighty, Amazons and Greys from fifty to seventy, conures from twenty-five to forty, and cockatiels from fifteen to thirty. The larger parrots are likely to have two or more human families. I suspect that individual birds who gain the reputation of being mean have suffered immensely from changes in their environment and in the way they relate to their human companions. My heart aches for those birds who recall a happier time than their old age in homes where they are not loved.

I will not live another forty years, so I have provided for Cosmo in my will. Still I worry about whether her new people will dote on her the way I have. I worry too about whether I have loved her too much, about whether I've led her to expect unreasonable affection from her future human family. Will she be welcomed into their conversations, encouraged to play "telephone," allowed some independence in their house? Will they talk with her, whistle with her, laugh at her jokes, and cuddle her at bedtime? I hope that by giving Cosmo a happy life I have given her the ability to bring happiness into the lives of others, who will in turn love her. Maybe that is the only way we can prepare our pets, and our young humans, to take on this world after we older folks leave it.

What will Cosmo remember of her life with me? I imagine she will remember that she lived in a house with dogs and a human there for her entertainment, that she often had human company, that she had squirrels and birds outside her window, that she had plenty of freedom from her cage, that she had all the peanuts she wanted, that she got kisses on her beak and on her feathers and on her feet, and that she had lots of cuddling. I fear she will also remember the joys of making sawdust out of baseboards, taking apart pens, eyeliners, and lipsticks, and exploring the insides of cabinets. I hope she will remember that when she talked people responded to her.

It is true that we humans keep parrots for our pleasure and not theirs. We are the conquerors of the land community, and we have been using animals for our pleasure for millennia. But even if, in the twenty-first century, we feel guilt over our destruction of Eden, the time has long passed for us to return to the wild all the animals—companion animals and beasts of burden—we have integrated into our lives. We can no more return dogs to their native habitats than we can reverse the evolution of pigs and cows.

Our human existence is intricately entwined with that of our fellow residents of the earth and has been for 6,000 years. Think of birds, dogs, cats, cows, pigs, goats, horses, sheep, donkeys, mules, deer, elephants, llamas, camels, monkeys, apes, dolphins, whales, oxen, bison, water buffalo, reindeer, yak, mink, fox, ferrets, rabbits, guinea pigs, mice, rats, seals, pigeons, falcons, hawks, eagles, chickens, turkeys, geese, snakes, turtles, goldfish, and the many other animals we humans have domesticated or tamed or kept as pets. We have trained these animals to work for us, transport us, protect us, and guard our possessions. We have bred them to feed us and clothe us. And we have kept them as companions to furnish us with affection.

Those we keep as companions we name, symbolically removing them from their natural habitat, whatever that may have been, and making them part of our human families. My friends have included KitKat Mitchell, Cowboy Bertsch, Ziggy Dingus, Barney Beckmann, Frosty and Cheerio Fischer, Deli and Muggins Shehane, Kazoo Lambert, Coco Bradley, Beaumont Brooks, Amadeus and Ludwig Cofer, Calico Craige, Greta Johnson, Scruffy Ledet, and Snowflake Ledet. Snowflake is a guinea pig. The others are dogs, cats, and birds. I have named my own dogs Zorro, Coco, Bandit, Sugar Bear, Holly, Blanche, Daisy, Kaylee, and Mary.

There must be a need deep within the human psyche to name, touch, hold, and cuddle our non-human fellow residents of the earth, at least the individuals who strike us as cute. We enjoy taming them, touching them, loving them, and getting them to love us. Why is that? What is the appeal of petting a bird or a dog or a cat or a guinea pig?

I believe the appeal is the emotional satisfaction we humans gain from feeling, for a transitory moment, that we are no longer conquerors of the land community but rather plain members and citizens of it.

Our conquest of the land community has endangered all its inhabitants. Now there is reason to worry that the current popularity of the African Grey is imperiling the species. The International Union for the Conservation of Nature and Natural Resources estimates that illicit parrot traders are reducing the total population of Greys in their native African habitats by 21 per cent annually. The trapping and transportation of the birds yields high mortality, and the pursuit of them destroys their nesting sites. In 2007, the IUCN for the first time listed the African Grey Parrot as "Near Threatened" on its Red List of Threatened Species, because of both the unlawful capture of the parrots and the disruption of their habitat. The Convention on International Trade in Endangered Species—signed by the United States, Western European nations, and African nations, including Congo—now prohibits the importing of African Greys into Europe and the United States, as does the Wild Bird Conservation Act.

Yet the illegal and unethical commerce continues. And anybody purchasing a wild-caught parrot is supporting this nefarious business. He or she is not only encouraging poaching but also subjecting an animal to captivity who has been accustomed to life in the wild.

The human should be locked up, not the unfortunate parrot. The breeding of parrots is an entirely different endeavor. African Greys hatched in captivity and hand-raised by their breeders grow up accustomed to life indoors, to interaction with humans, and to an environment loaded with language and other non-jungle sounds and sights. They become good pets because they develop a fondness for us, who take care of them, and because they adapt well to our homes. Although Greys are not yet domesticated, in that they have the same genetic make-up as their wild cousins from whom they are only a few generations removed, they do become very tame. It is our responsibility as their people to keep them tame and happy, by providing them a living space stimulating and gratifying enough to keep their minds active, their spirits up, and their social skills honed.

I have written this book, *Conversations with Cosmo*, to show the intellectual and linguistic achievements of one wonderful African Grey Parrot, in the belief that the more we humans learn about the mental capabilities of African Greys and of all our other non-human fellow residents of the earth the more vigilant we will be about their welfare.

There are six and a half billion of us humans on a planet that everywhere feels the effect of our activity—in the rain forests of Central Africa, across the deserts of the Sahara, on the glaciers of Antarctica. If we define *wilderness* as areas where humans have yet to trespass, there isn't any, not anymore, for we humans have impacted the habitats of just about all of our non-human fellow residents of the earth. We are methodically excluding from our expanding cities and towns all the wild animals who once claimed the turf as their own, leaving them to forage on smaller and smaller bits of forest between freeways. We are gradually silencing the calls of the awakening birds in the morning. The Audubon Society reports that population growth and habitat destruction have caused the decline of over half the migratory songbird species in the United States. Overfishing and industrial pollution have disrupted the ecosystems of our lakes, rivers, and oceans, sometimes irreversibly.

We humans are so numerous that our decisions about what to harvest, cultivate, mine, log, gather, hunt, capture, or fish, and how much, where to live and where not to live, and what parts of the planet to maintain in "natural" condition affect the atmosphere, the hydrosphere, the lithosphere, and the biosphere. Our decisions affect the nature of "nature." They determine the condition of the whole planet and of every creature on it.

Cosmo does not know that human activity is threatening the survival of her species. But she can teach us that we humans are not alone in having a lively inner life, that she and countless fellow residents of the earth have thoughts and feelings. Maybe we will make some wiser decisions now that we know her personally.

> COSMO: "Cosmo is a good bird."
> BJC: "Yes, Cosmo is a good good bird."
> COSMO: "Cosmo is a good good good birdy!"
> BJC: "Yes, yes, yes, oh, yes!"

Back in cage
Ball
Bark *woo woo woo*
Be back soon
Betty Jean be back soon
Betty Jean be back soon,
  okay?
Betty Jean, come here!
Betty Jean go in a car
Betty Jean go to work?
Betty Jean gonna go to
  work
Betty Jean has clothes
Betty Jean have to leave
Betty Jean is a bad bird!
Betty Jean wanna cuddle?
Betty Jean wanna go to
  kitchen?
Betty Jean wanna kiss a
  beak?
Betty Jean wanna kiss

feathers?
Betty Jean wanna
  shower?
Betty Jean wanna whis-
  tle?
Betty Jean's bedroom
Betty Jean's bathroom
Bird
Birdies
Birdy
Birdy has feathers
Birdy has feathers and a
  beak
Book
Bye
Come
Come here
Come here, okay?
Come here, please
Come here, Mary
Come here, doggies

Come on
Come up here
Come, Mary (whistles for Mary)
Cosmo
Cosmo and Betty Jean go to kitchen
Cosmo and Betty Jean wanna cuddle?
Cosmo and Betty Jean wanna dance?
Cosmo and Betty Jean wanna talk?
Cosmo and Betty Jean wanna whistle?
Cosmo bad bird?
Cosmo bad bird—go back in cage
Cosmo go back in cage?
Cosmo be a good bird—okay?
Cosmo don't bite—okay?
Cosmo don't wanna be a good bird
Cosmo don't wanna go to kitchen
Cosmo go back in cage
Cosmo has a beak
Cosmo has feathers
Cosmo has feathers and a

beak
Cosmo has feet
Cosmo is a bird
Cosmo is a birdy
Cosmo is a good bird
Cosmo is a good birdy
Cosmo is a good girl
Cosmo is a good good bird
Cosmo is a good good girl
Cosmo is a good good good bird
Cosmo is a good good good good bird
Cosmo is what a bird!
Cosmo s... a squirrel
Cosmo s... a birdy
Cosmo wanna be a good bird
Cosmo wanna cuddle
Cosmo wanna go for a walk? Okay? Noooo! Cosmo is a bird.
Cosmo wanna go in a car, okay?
Cosmo wanna go to bathroom
Cosmo wanna go to bed
Cosmo wanna go to Betty Jean's bathroom
Cosmo wanna go to Betty

Jean's bedroom
Cosmo wanna go to Betty
   Jean's desk
Cosmo wanna go to Betty
   Jean room
Cosmo wanna go to Betty
   Jean's room
Cosmo wanna go to
   Cosmo room
Cosmo wanna go to work
Cosmo wanna go up—
   okay?
Cosmo wanna good kiss
Cosmo wanna grape
Cosmo wanna orange
Cosmo wanna peanut
Cosmo wanna peanut,
   please
Cosmo wanna play
Cosmo wanna poop
Cosmo wanna shower
Cosmo wanna shower
Cosmo wanna talk
Cosmo wanna water
Cosmo wanna water for
   cage
Cosmo wanna whistle
Dog
Doggies
Doggies bark

Doggies be back soon
Doggies go for a walk?
Doggies wanna go for a
   walk
Doggies wanna go in a car
Doggies, come here!
Doggy
Don't bite!
Feathers
Fine
Fine, thank you
Go up here
Good bird
Good girl
Good morning
Good night
Good shower! Wow!
Good whistle
Goodbye
Have to leave?
Hello
Here are you?
Here I am
Hi
Hi, Mary
How are you?
I am here
I love you
I love you!
I wanna go in a car

I wanna go to work
I wanna kiss
I wanna shower and a
   peanut
Kay is a doggy
Kaylee is a doggy
Kerry is a doggy
Let go
Let go please. Thank you
Let's go
Let's go to Betty Jean
   room
Let's go to kitchen
Let's talk
Let's wanna cuddle
Look!
Look, squirrel
Mary go in a car?
Mary has feathers! No!
Mary is a doggy
Move!
No
No more peanut
No, Mary!
No, no more
No, no more kiss
No, No, bad bird
No, no, no!
Oh good
Okay

Okay?
Okay, Cosmo
Ow!
Peanut
Play ball
Please
Shower for Betty Jean
   room
Squirrel
Squirrelly
Stay here!
Step up
Step up please
Step up, step up up up—
   Please
Telephone for Betty Jean
Telephone for bird!
Telephone for good bird!
Telephone!
Thank you
That hurt!
That hurt?
That's bark
That's bad doggy!
That's doggy bark
That's paper for Cosmo's
   poop
That's poop
That's shower for Betty
   Jean

That's telebird

That's television

There you are

Time for shower and a
    peanut

Time for shower and a
    peanut for Cosmo

Time for shower for Betty
    Jean

Time for shower for Cosmo

Time for shower and a
    peanut for Cosmo in
    Cosmo room, okay?

Time to go to bed

Time to go to bed for Cosmo

Up

Wanna apple

Wanna be a good bird

Wanna cuddle

Wanna cuddle?

Wanna dance?

Wanna go back in cage

Wanna go to bed?

Wanna go to kitchen?

Wanna go up

Wanna go up here

Wanna kiss (followed by:
    kissing sounds)

Wanna kiss?

Wanna play?

Wanna poop

Wanna shower and a
    peanut

Water

We're gonna go in a car

We're gonna go to Betty
    Jean bedroom

We're gonna go to Cosmo
    room

We're gonna go to kitchen

We're gonna have com-
    pany

What a bird!

What a girl!

What a good girl!

What are you doing?

What do you want?

What doing?

What's Cosmo? Cosmo is
    a bird

What's Cosmo? Cosmo is
    a birdy

What?

What's that?

What's that? That's birdy

What's that? That's
    Cosmo

Where are you?

Where gonna go?

Where wanna gonna go?

Conversations With Cosmo

Where's Cosmo?

Woo woo woo! That's
   doggy bark

Wow

Wow! Good shower!

Wow! Good kiss!

Yes

Yoohoo

You have reached 935-4362

You have reached Betty

Jean!

You have reached Cosmo!

You have reached
   Cosmo—Hello

You have reached good
   bird!

You wanna kiss?

You wanna dance?

You wanna go to kitchen?

Forty-Four Tips for Living with an African Grey
(Or Things I Have Learned from Cosmo about Loving an African Grey)

GOLDEN RULE: *If you love your African Grey Parrot, respect your bird, talk to your bird, stimulate your bird intellectually and socially, take good care of your bird, and make him or her an important part of your life, he or she—but for simplicity's sake let's call the bird "she" and name her "Pajarita"—will love you back. Everything else on this list of things you can do to have a great parrot companion follows from the Golden Rule.*

1. If the African Grey Parrot you acquire is a baby, do not take her home until she can eat on her own.

2. If you like, you can name your baby as soon as you make your selection, so that he or she comes to know his or her name right away. If you pick a gender-neutral name then you won't risk naming him or her a gender-inappropriate name (if that matters to you).

    If you are giving a bird her second or third home, don't rename her. She'll have enough adjustment problems without having to get a new identity.

3. Buy your cage (or cages) and set it (or them) up before you bring Pajarita home. Buy a small car cage for travel (home from the breeder or the pet store, to and from the

veterinarian's office, to and from friends' houses for dinner parties, etc.).

4. African Greys need at least one big cage, approximately 22" x 24" x 53," with playscape on top. You should put some toys in it for Pajarita to investigate when you're not around. She will eventually destroy them, but that's what they are there for. Be prepared to buy new toys on a regular basis, and new perches. Concrete perches are good for Pajarita's toenails, but they are less mobile than rope perches, which can be placed at angles in the cage. I suggest you get at least one of each for each big cage.

Position the perches so that Pajarita doesn't poop in her water or food dishes.

5. Find a good location for Pajarita's roost cage. Since that's the cage where Pajarita will sleep, be sure that the room can be darkened or the cage covered at night, because Pajarita will need 10-12 hours of uninterrupted sleep.

If Pajarita spends most of her time in her roost cage, it should be situated where she has lots of natural light from outdoors and where she has a variety of activities to observe when she is locked up. Ideally, during the daytime if she is alone in the house, the cage should be moved near a window, so that Pajarita can watch birds, squirrels, and people outside.

The cage should also be where the temperature doesn't get below 69 degrees or above 80 degrees.

The cage should be where Pajarita will not be bored, where she can listen to and talk with your (her) family. The large cage will come with wheels, so you may want to roll it into a room where there's lots of action during the day and then roll it into a quiet room at Pajarita's bedtime.

6. If you can afford to get several cages, you can keep Pajarita with you when you are in different parts of the house: for example, in your living room, in your bedroom, in your study, or wherever you spend lots of time. Pajarita will want to be with you, and the more time she spends with you the more she will talk and the more affectionate she will become.

Remember that African Greys are flock animals, and Pajarita will want to be with her flock: you and the other family members, human and non-human.

7. Be sure that your breeder or your pet store allows you to have Pajarita examined by an avian veterinarian before you complete your purchase.

8. Have Pajarita sexed. The vet can send a feather to a DNA lab to find out whether the bird is a male or a female. (Obviously, I thought Cosmo was a male when I named her.) The vet and you should know Pajarita's sex in case of future health problems.

9. Buy parrot pellets from your pet store for Pajarita's cage(s). They will provide her the nutrition she needs. Then be prepared to supplement her diet with dry roasted unsalted peanuts, corn on the cob, squash, cranberries, green beans, okra, orange slices, watermelon, pasta (uncooked and cooked), and any other fruits and vegetables you yourself are eating—except for avocado. No avocado!

Avocado is toxic to parrots. So are alcohol, chocolate, and caffeine. Salty and greasy foods are likewise bad for their health.

You can keep packages of frozen mixed vegetables so that you can give Pajarita a variety of foods.

10. Give away all your Teflon products, all of them. Teflon emits a gas when overheated that will quickly kill your bird. Since you never know when you might accidentally overheat your Teflon pans, just get rid of them. That's a small price to pay for your bird's life.

11. Throw away all your ammonia-based cleaning products, and buy vinegar-based cleansers instead. Vinegar-based products work fine for cleaning cages (and once you bring Pajarita into your life you won't have time to clean much else).

12. Get some sort of plastic mat to place under the cage if the cage is on carpet. If the cage is on linoleum, tile, or hardwood, your life will be easier.

13. Before you bring Pajarita home, lock your dogs in the bedroom.

14. After you bring Pajarita home and put her safely into her cage, you can introduce her to your other family members—dogs, children, and humans. But *be careful!* Although my dogs now get along well with Cosmo, they certainly would have liked a taste of her when I brought her into the family.

15. Be especially careful not to let Pajarita too close to children's faces, or to anybody's face, for that matter. *A bird does not belong in the vicinity of eyes.* She may become frightened and bite.

16. As soon as possible establish a routine for Pajarita's care and feeding.

Put Pajarita to bed at approximately the same time every night. Say—even before Pajarita can talk—"Time to go to sleep" or "Time to go to bed," followed by "I love you" and "Pajarita is a good bird!"

In the morning, greet Pajarita and let her out of the cage. She will probably want to do her big morning poop outside the cage, since she will not do it where she sleeps. Try to train her to climb immediately onto the perch on the playscape above her cage and do it onto the papers from that perch. When she does it, you can say, "Pajarita poop" or "That's poop" so that she will learn the word. She will need it.

Spend some time when Pajarita wakes up to talk with her and to handle her. And then give her food and fresh water. Most cages have three dishes: one for water, one for pellet food, and one for goodies, like corn on the cob, peanuts, or grapes.

17. Play physically with Pajarita every day to keep her tame and accustomed to your touch.

18. Clean the cage (or cages) once a week, and change the newspaper at least every two days. You may want to subscribe to *The New York Times* to keep enough newspaper handy.

19. Weigh Pajarita regularly on a small scale to determine whether she is gaining or losing weight as she grows.

20. Know that Pajarita may bite you on occasion, and learn to recognize by her body posture when she is

127

preparing to bite. Then avoid the situation.

If Pajarita bites you, or somebody else, say sharply, "Pajarita is a bad, bad bird! Go back in cage!" Then put her into her cage and ignore her for a while.

Never, ever strike your bird—even if she bites you. Striking your bird will make her fear you for the rest of her life. It will destroy her trust in you and possibly in all other humans. Birds are not mammals, and they must not be disciplined like dogs.

21. Do not enter Pajarita's cage when Pajarita is in it. Her cage is her sanctuary. She will naturally bite when she sees her sanctuary invaded. If you want her to come out of her cage, just leave the cage door open. Unless she is fearful of a situation she'll happily emerge on her own.

22. If you become afraid of Pajarita, you should probably not keep her. Give her back to the breeder or the pet store, or find somebody who will love her.

23. You may need to throw a small towel over Pajarita to catch her if she runs away from you, or if you and the vet need to hold her. Then hold her very, very gently. Her bone structure is fragile.

24. Immediately, teach Pajarita to "Step up"—that is, to hop on your hand. You can do this by putting your left hand in front of Pajarita and putting your right hand behind her to gently nudge her if necessary. Practice "step up" regularly.

25. Normally, African Greys don't start talking until they are a year old. But they can whistle at a very young age. So when Pajarita starts whistling, whistle back.

You can teach Pajarita to wolf-whistle—*whee whew*—and to call your dogs. Pajarita will start mimicking the sounds of birds and squirrels, as well as the fire engine sirens, the doorbell, the smoke alarm, and the other household appliances.

26. Talk to Pajarita, in simplified language, from the day you bring her into your home. For example, say, "I love you" when you're showing her affection; say, Pajarita is a good bird" when she is being a good bird. She will be absorbing your language for six months before she starts to talk.

27. Speak of yourself in third person, so that Pajarita can learn your name. For example, you can say, "Betty Jean wanna shower" (if your name is Betty Jean).

28. When you offer Pajarita food, ask her if she would like it. For example, say, "Pajarita wanna peanut?" "Pajarita wanna orange?"

When you ask her to go with you, say, "Pajarita wanna go with me?" Or (if your name is Betty Jean) "Pajarita wanna go with Betty Jean?"

Pajarita will soon learn the difference between a declarative sentence and a question. If you're telling Pajarita where she is going to go, say "Pajarita gonna go in a car" or "Pajarita go to kitchen."

29. Use relatively few words and a simple syntax to speak to Pajarita. Here are some examples:

Step up.
Go up.
No
Good

Bad
Wanna
Go to
Where
Here
I love you
What's that?
That's _____
Okay
Don't
Gonna
For
Time for _____
Wow
With
And
More

30. When Pajarita starts talking, she will repeat what she has heard you say to her, and probably in the right context.

Pajarita will practice her language when she is by herself. She will try out new words and new sounds. You may hear her say when she first awakens, "Pajarita is a bird! Pajarita is a good bird! Hello. Where are you? I'm here!"

31. Give Pajarita access to your company, when you have people over, so that she learns social skills. Perhaps you can move her cage into the living room or the dining room. Encourage your friends to whistle to her and to talk with her—but not crowd around her cage. She will soon want to join in the fun.

32. *Do not let anybody use bad language in your house.* If Pajarita picks up bad words, she will not be acceptable to some of your guests, and then she will not be in-

vited to parties—yours or theirs. Even more importantly, she will not be loved by her future family (or families).

Greys can live fifty years or more, and they are likely to have several families in their lifetimes. You must make Pajarita into a good bird with polite language to ensure that she is lovable for her whole life. You want her to be happy when you are no longer there to care for her.

33. Spend quality time with Pajarita, talking directly to her, answering her questions, making her feel that you two are communicating. *Do not ignore her when she is talking to you.* You must let her know that talking means communicating and that talking brings results. If Pajarita says, "Pajarita wanna go to kitchen," you must answer her: either "Okay, Pajarita and Betty Jean go to kitchen" (if your name is Betty Jean) or "No, Pajarita stay here, okay?"

34. Be funny with Pajarita. When the phone rings, you can shout "Telephone for Pajarita!" She'll learn to laugh like you and at appropriate times, and she'll begin making up her own jokes.

35. To keep Pajarita happy, you must give her a lively social and intellectual life. That means that *you must include her in your activities.* She is a very smart bird, and if she is not with her flock, if she does not have lots of different things to think about and to observe, if she gets bored or unhappy or lonely, she will feather-pick. Then you will have a big problem.

Feather-picking, though it occasionally results from physical ailments, is usually a sign of boredom, unhappiness, and loneliness.

36. If you cannot keep Pajarita happy, if you are too busy to make her an important part of your life, you should find another home for her. *Keeping an unhappy bird—or keeping a bird unhappy—is cruelty.*

In the rain forest, where Pajarita's ancestors lived, African Greys have exciting lives—foraging for food, escaping from predators, looking for mates, building nests, flying with each other, etc. Those of us who keep pet birds must ensure that they get plenty of stimulation and affection.

37. After Pajarita feels comfortable with you, you can handle her, caress her feathers, cuddle her. You might want to do this at the end of the day when she is tired. Say, "Pajarita wanna cuddle," and bring her onto your lap. If she starts to bite, she's telling you she doesn't want to cuddle. Just put her back into her cage.

38. Pajarita may want simply to be with you. You can put her on the back of your chair while you're reading, and she'll preen happily in your presence.

39. Take Pajarita out with you in the car. She will probably love the excursions. But never let her out of her car cage. That's dangerous for her, and for you, and for oncoming traffic.

40. Give Pajarita as much time outside the cage when you're home as possible. She will need at least two hours of independence every day. Even if she is just sitting on the back of your chair, she will enjoy the freedom from her cage.

41. Keep Pajarita's feathers clipped, so that she won't fly into a fan, against a window, or through a door to the

outside. You'll give Pajarita much more time outside her cage if you are not worrying about where she wants to fly.

42. Try not to fret when Pajarita picks at your baseboards, crawls into your cupboards, opens your drawers, and sticks her beak into every nook and cranny of your house. She is curious, she is intelligent, and she wants to have fun. That's why you will love her.

43. Put Pajarita into your will. When you depart this life, you will want Pajarita to go to good people who will care for her the way you have cared for her. You want her to remember you fondly, but be happy in her new environment.

44. Remember the Golden Rule.

Index

INDEX